D0394485

OPEN AND UTILITY TRAINING

The Motivational Method

OPEN AND UTILITY TRAINING

The Motivational Method

Jack and Wendy Volhard

HOWELL
BOOK HOUSE

New York

Maxwell Macmillan Canada
Toronto

Maxwell Macmillan International
New York   Oxford   Singapore   Sydney

Howell Book House
Macmillan Publishing Company
866 Third Avenue
New York, NY 10022

Maxwell Macmillan Canada, Inc.
1200 Eglinton Avenue East
Suite 200
Don Mills, Ontario M3C 3N1

Macmillan Publishing Company is part of the Maxwell Communication Group of Companies.

Library of Congress Cataloging-in-Publication Data

Volhard, Joachim.
    Open and utility training: the motivational method / Jack and Wendy Volhard.
        p.   cm.
    Includes bibliographical references.
    ISBN 0-87605-755-5
    1. Dogs—Obedience trials—Open classes.   2. Dogs—Obedience trials—Utility classes.   3. Dogs—Training.   4. Dogs—Behavior.
    I. Volhard, Wendy.   II. Title.   III. Title: Motivational method.
SF425.7.V65   1992   91–32589
636.7′088′7—dc20   CIP

Macmillan books are available at special discounts for bulk purchases for sales promotions, premiums, fund-raising, or educational use. For details, contact:

Special Sales Director
Macmillan Publishing Company
866 Third Avenue
New York, NY 10022

10 9 8 7 6 5 4 3 2 1

Printed in the United States of America

In memory of the Landseer Newfoundlands
who taught us how to train:

Rivendell's Cassandra, CDX;
Can. OT Ch. Rivendell's Cato, UD, VB, WRD;
Henna von Schartenberg (Heidi), UD;
Basso vom Bottwartal, CDX;
Rivendell's Arin, CD; and
Rivendell's Dingo, CDX, Can. CD, WRD

Contents

Part III.   Utility Training

About the Authors

Jack Volhard has authored over 100 articles for various dog publications and is the recipient of five awards from the Dog Writers' Association of America (DWAA). He is the senior author of *Training Your Dog: The Step-by-Step Manual* (Howell Book House, 1983), named Best Care and Training Book for 1983 by the DWAA; *Teaching Dog Obedience Classes: The Manual for Instructors* (Howell Book House, 1986), acclaimed as "the state-of-the-art text for instructors"; *What All Good Dogs Should Know: The Sensible Way to Train* (Howell Book House, 1991); the videotapes *Teaching Dog Obedience Classes: Foundation Training* (1988); *Open Training: The Teaching Phase* (1990); *Utility Training: The Teaching Phase* (1990) and *Motivational Retrieve: Teaching, Practicing, Testing* (1991).

Jack has been an AKC Obedience judge since 1973, a member of the National Association of Dog Obedience Instructors since 1971 and a member of the Association of Dog Obedience Clubs and Judges.

Wendy Volhard developed the most widely used system for evaluating and selecting puppies, and her film *Puppy Aptitude Testing* was named Best Film on Dogs for 1981 by the DWAA. Her four-part series "Motivating Your Dog for Competition," published by *Off-Lead* magazine, was named Best Series for 1981 by the DWAA. She had formulated a balanced, home-made dog food; gives seminars on behavior, instructing, nutrition and training and has lectured at the prestigious Natural History Musuem in London.

Wendy is a member of the Animal Behavior Society, the Delta Society and the Advisory Board of the North American Wildlife Foundation.

The Volhards, internationally known as "trainers of trainers," are also active exhibitors who have obtained over forty Obedience titles, multiple Highs in Trial and Dog World Awards of Canine Distinction with their Landseer Newfoundlands, Standard Wirehaired Dachshund, Yorkshire Terrier, Labrador Retriever and German Shepherd Dog.

Over the past twenty-five years, through their training classes, lectures, weekend seminars and five-day training camps, they have taught over 10,000 people how to communicate with their dog, how to make training fun for both owner and dog and how to achieve a mutually rewarding relationship.

Acknowledgments

OUR THANKS to those who gave their time and energy to participate in the photographic session for this book:

Diane Betelak and Alex (Standard Poodle)
Christine Duval and Tops (Standard Wirehaired Dachshund)
Gary Gordon and Murphy (Golden Retriever)
Joan Greenwald and Atlas and Balsam
(Landseer Newfoundlands)
JoAnne Klinetop and Sesha (Golden Retriever)
Annie Perrino and Keke (Bernese Mountain Dog)
Jane Stansbury and Trouble (Labrador Retriever)
Lucille Staub and Twinkie (Silky Terrier)
and part of the Volhard family of dogs
Bean (Labrador Retriever)
Demi, Diggy, and Manfred
(Standard Wirehaired Dachshunds)
Gocelyn and Pinky (Landseer Newfoundlands)
Katharina (German Shepherd Dog)

Foreword

WELCOME to the Motivational Method, an approach to training for people who like their dogs and who have them first and foremost as pets and companions. It dates back to 1970 and was developed as an instructing method to help those with little or no experience in training a dog. The techniques are simple, flexible and imaginative, and can be readily tailored to specific needs.

The Motivational Method is based on twenty-five years of research on dog behavior and uses the latest findings on how dogs learn. Every exercise is logically structured into a series of step-by-step sequences, each one readily mastered by your dog as progress is made in training. This method relies on *positive* reinforcement and uses your dog's instincts and strenghts to teach what you want the dog to learn. Learning becomes easy and enjoyable, as complex chains of behaviors are mastered. Starting with the companion dog whose owner just wants basic control, training levels progress through Open and Utility training for AKC competition.

The relationship between man and dog is complex and often suffers from poor communication. Blending human and canine psychology into a carefully structured program, the Motivational Method bridges the gap between the species. Training results in a dog who believes he can succeed, a belief that is crucial because without it, the dog cannot continue to learn and perform in a reliable, motivated fashion. As the work becomes increasingly demanding, the dog accepts the challenge. The dog has been taught to succeed, and at no time has been placed in a position of failure. The same applies to you, the trainer.

Recognizing that clear and congruent communication is necessary for successful training, the Motivational Method places great emphasis on teaching the handler the skills of body posture, leash handling, tone of voice and an understanding of dog behavior, as well as the mechanics for every exercise. "Success breeds success" is an old saying and one that applies to this method. With the ultimate goal of an enthusiastic, reliable and precise dog, the Motivational Method gives you the tools to achieve that goal.

PART I

Behavior, Motivation and Training

1

The Three Phases
of Training

---

*With a sweet tongue and kindness, you can drag an
elephant by a hair.*

Persian proverb

THE MOTIVATIONAL METHOD consists of
three phases of training:

1. teaching
2. practicing
3. testing

Although you may not have looked at it that way, in your
Novice training, more than likely, you already followed a similar approach. Even so, there are a few refinements and dis-
tinctions you may not have thought of before that we are going
to outline for you.

THE TEACHING PHASE

In the *teaching phase* we teach Konrad the particular response we want him to learn. First, we break down the exercise into tiny components, each one small enough so that he can readily understand it. Using such a step-by-step approach eliminates confusion or doubt on the part of the dog during the teaching process. It also enhances and maintains motivation throughout the training. Konrad almost cannot help but be successful, and success is still the best motivator of them all.

First impressions leave the most lasting impact, and how Konrad *perceives* the introduction to obedience or a new exercise determines his outlook. Konrad's attitude toward training and what we are trying to teach him is shaped by the first progression. If the introduction is pleasant and nonthreatening, he will enjoy the activity and will be a willing and enthusiastic student. If it is unpleasant and anxiety producing, chances are he will dislike it and resist training.

In teaching a new exercise to our dogs we use the following model to avoid unnecessary stress and anxiety:

1. show
2. induce
3. induce/compel
4. if necessary, compel.

Show

The first time we introduce Konrad to a new exercise or a new sequence of an exercise, we show him exactly what we want. For example, to teach him to lie down on command, we first physically place him in the down position with the command "Down." Or to teach him to go over the High Jump, we show what to do by going with him or guiding him over the jump. This sequence is repeated for a total of twenty-five times over the course of several sessions.

Induce

For the next step we try to elicit a voluntary response from Konrad through the use of an object of attraction, such as a

4

In the show sequence, Bean's front feet are lifted into the begging position . . .

and he is placed in the down position.

piece of food, a ball, a stick or a toy—whatever attracts him. In the example of the Down, we show the object to Konrad, then lower it to the ground with the command "Down," and let him have the object after he has responded correctly. With

With a small dog . . .

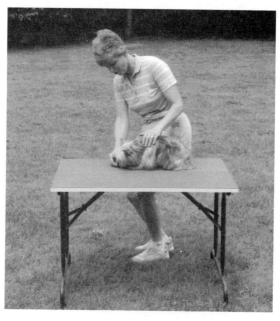

this exercise can be done on a table.

a small dog, this sequence can be done on a table. Repeat for a total of twenty-five times over the course of several sessions.

It is at this step that he becomes familiar with the command for Down. Although some dogs learn the command during this sequence, most require further training.

The purpose of Obedience training is to have your dog respond *when* and *because* you give a command. Even though Konrad may perform an exercise because he enjoys it, he also has to learn to respond even when he does not particularly feel like it. The third step of the model lays the groundwork for teaching him to obey the command at any time.

Induce/compel

We now combine inducement in the form of an object of attraction with compulsion, which can range from the really unpleasant, such as a slight pressure on the dog's collar, to the physical discomfort produced by a check. In our example of the Down, we induce Konrad with an object while at the same time applying downward pressure on the collar saying, "Down." Pressure on the collar is *essential* here because it is the foundation for the next step, and the dog learns to accept compulsion as part of the teaching process. This sequence is also repeated twenty-five times over the course of several sessions.

If necessary, compel

We now rely on compulsion alone to get the desired response. Konrad has had at least seventy-five repetitions of the command and has some idea what we want. We give the command and at the same time apply downward pressure on the collar. Since he has already gone through the first three steps of the model, he willingly lies down.

In the final step of teaching him to lie down on command, we quietly say "Down" and give him a chance to respond. If nothing happens, we check straight down. That sequence is repeated until Konrad lies down on command.

Once Konrad understands an exercise, we are ready to go on to the *practicing* phase.

With an object, fingers through the collar . . .

and downward pressure on the collar, Bean lies down.

THE PRACTICING PHASE

In this phase we increase the complexity of the exercises to teach Konrad to concentrate on what he is doing and to build confidence.

This is the most exciting part of training because you can observe your dog "thinking" and trying to work out what it is you want. One of the most rewarding training experiences is when you see the "aha" response, when the penny finally drops and the dog in effect says "now I have figured it out" and does it correctly without any help from you.

The practicing phase is based on two assumptions:

With two fingers through the collar and downward pressure, Bean lies down.

Bean lies down on command.

1. New situations, such as a dog show, can produce stress and anxiety, especially if the dog is shy, which undermine Konrad's confidence to the point where he feels "I can't do it." In this phase we work on building that confidence, mainly through the introduction of increasingly, difficult distractions, so that the dog learns the exercise can be correctly performed under almost all conditions.

At the same time, you, the handler, gain the confidence and conviction that your dog can do it, which in some cases is even more important than the dog's confidence. Many handlers become excessively nervous when they exhibit their dogs. Some walk entirely differently than they do normally; other develop spasms and twitches; for others still their voices change. Whatever it may be, this hopelessly confuses their dogs, who at best turn in a poor performance and at worst fail to qualify. Such a "failure," then serves as justification for trainers becoming nervous because their dogs have just demonstrated how unreliable they are, creating a vicious cycle.

Adequate preparation is necessary to deal with this nervousness and to help control it. Distraction training, which teaches Konrad to concentrate on what he is supposed to do without becoming distracted, is a critical component.

Part of that preparation includes taking the dog to different locations to train and practice. When we teach Konrad a new exercise we start in a *familiar* area free from distractions so that we are his center of attention. As he catches on, we then take him to an *unfamiliar* area free from distractions, which is the first step to performing under new and different conditions. During this time Konrad also goes to training class where he learns to respond in a familiar setting with distractions. His education is rounded out by going to unfamiliar locations with distractions, including matches.

When you take Konrad to a new location, it will take him some time to get used to it. That time will become shorter and shorter as he gains experience working in different locations and around various distractions. When you take him to his first Trial, only you will know whether your preparation has been adequate and how much time he needs to orient himself to perform to his potential.

Deep down in the inner recesses of that little brain, lurk a variety of unacceptable responses.

Once Konrad has demonstrated his reliability under those conditions, he is ready to go.

2. Deep down in the inner recesses of the dog's brain lurks a variety of unacceptable responses. Even though Konrad may always have done it correctly at home and in class, take him to a Trial and he will surprise you with ingenuity. For example, for the Retrieve Over the High Jump, Konrad can think of a number of unacceptable responses: over the jump and back around it either to the right or the left; around the jump on the way out, either to the right or the left; over the jump, standing over the dumbbell; over the jump and returning only part way; not jumping at all, etc., etc.

During this phase of training we want to bring these responses out in the open so that we can eliminate them, rather than wait until they surface at a Trial. It has been our observation that dogs become especially imaginative when in the ring. Perhaps performing in front of spectators triggers this heretofore dormant creativity. Or the dogs are just confused and start to engage in random behaviors.

Whatever the answer, Konrad needs to learn to perform

First degree distraction with distractor standing two feet from the dumbbell.

11

the exercises the way the Obedience Regulations require them to be done—the correct way—even at Trials.

To this end we introduce distraction training in a structured and systematic way. Distractions are introduced over the course of three to five sessions or weeks, depending on the dog's coping ability. They range from easy to difficult, or what we call first degree to third degree. A shy dog will take a little longer than a bold dog to master this part of training.

First degree distractions are *visual* such as an object or a person. For example, once Konrad knows how to retrieve, you are ready to introduce first degree distractions. Throw the dumbbell and have a distractor—who can be a family member, training partner or fellow student at class—stand two feet from the dumbbell, facing the dog, and then give the command. Your distractor assumes a nonthreatening posture.

An entire series of first degree distractions would look something like this. The distractor stands about two feet away, then a little closer, then over the dumbbell; then he hides the dumbbell by standing with his back to the dog, blocking the dog's view, and lightly puts his foot on it. You can also use a chair and have your dog retrieve the dumbbell from under the chair and from the seat.

Second degree distractions are *visual* and *auditory*. The distractor now crouches and tries to distract the dog by lightly clapping hands and saying "here, puppy, puppy." The dog's name is *not* used.

The distractor tries to hide the dumbbell . . .   but Katharina is not fooled.

12

Second degree distraction with distractor encouraging dog to visit.

Third degree distractions are *sensory* or *tactile*, such as offering the dog an object of attraction or touching the dog.

Distraction training is equally important for the shy dog and the bold dog, to build confidence and to teach concentration, respectively, so both learn to respond correctly under different conditions.

During distraction training, you will see the following responses or variations thereof.

1. **Lack of Confidence**—Konrad starts but then backs off or avoids the distractor, meaning "I don't have the confidence to do this."

Third degree distraction with distractor using an object.

13

2. **Avoidance**—Konrad leaves altogether, meaning "I can't cope with this."

3. **Freezing**—Konrad does nothing, meaning "if I don't do anything maybe all of this will go away."

4. **Distraction**—Konrad goes to the distractor.

5. **Anticipation**—Konrad anticipates; meaning "I'm catching on, see how clever I am."

6. **Successful Completion**—Konrad does it correctly and that is when you stop for that session!

It is unlikely that you will see more than three or four responses from your dog, depending on your prior training and how your dog takes to distraction training. One remedy for each of these responses is described in the training chapters.

During distraction training, keep in mind that *any time you change the complexity of the exercise, it becomes a new exercise for the dog.* No, your dog is not defiant, stubborn or stupid, just confused about what you expect. Go back to the model and help your dog understand what it is you want.

By challenging Konrad to use his head, we intensify the strength of his responses and increase his confidence in his ability to perform under almost all conditions.

While using distraction training, it is also important to give Konrad a chance to work it out for himself. Don't be so

Just having fun.

quick to try and help him. At such times, Konrad's responses may be slow and you will be tempted to speed him up. *Don't* yield to the temptation. Just as in the teaching phase, when Konrad learns something new, we expect the response to be slow until he is sure he understands what to do. Be patient and let him try to figure out on his own how to do it correctly. Once he does, you will be pleasantly surprised by the intensity and reliability with which he responds.

A word of caution: While distraction training is exciting and fun, use common sense. If after several tries Konrad is not successful and becomes anxious about the exercise, stop. Ask yourself, "Does he have to do this in order to get a qualifying score?" If the answer is no, don't make an issue out of it! In the ring, chances are there will be no immediate distractions.

You will also have noticed that loud noises or anything else that could frighten, scare or startle a dog are not part of our repertoire of distractions. For example, we do not recommend such things as dropping chairs behind dogs on a Stay or banging pots and pans. Any potential benefit of these maneuvers is far outweighed by the potential damage. They quite literally could ruin a dog for life, so why take the chance? Distraction training is supposed to build the dog's confidence, not undermine it.

For the foundation of distraction training and more information, see *Teaching Dog Obedience Classes: The Manual for Instructors.*

THE TESTING PHASE

In the *testing phase,* handler and dog have to learn how the exercise has to be performed in the ring. You have to eliminate all the little body motions or extra commands you use during the teaching and practicing phases. Some of these have become so ingrained that you are no longer aware you are using them. If you are not sure what you are doing with your body when you are testing your dog, have someone watch you, or better still, have someone videotape you. The camera does not lie and you may be horrified by what you see.

Practice as though you are in the ring where you can't help your dog, where he has to respond without any assistance from you and where everyone is watching you. You also have to get your act together and learn how to control your emotions. (See Chapter 4, Stress and Your Dog.)

We are often told that dogs are "ringwise," that is, they perform fine at home, in class and at matches, but make mistakes at Trials and only at Trials. If Konrad knows the difference between a five dollar match and a twenty dollar Trial— you must have told him. How do you think you did that?

Konrad, in turn, has to learn that he is responsible for the correct response without any help from you, the handler. He learns this through practicing testing, the way it will be done in the ring. The judge says "forward . . . halt, etc." and no matter what Konrad does, at that moment there is nothing you can do about it. *That* is testing!

A final word about training your dog: Practice makes permanent; it does not make perfect. Only perfect practice makes perfect.

CONCLUSION

By using the Motivational Method, your dog enjoys the training and you enjoy teaching. That is motivation—not short-term obedience through fear, but long-term commitment through understanding.

2

Understanding
Your Dog

If our approach to training is based on moral ideas regarding punishment, reward, obedience, duty etc., we are bound to handle the dog in the wrong way.

Konrad Most

IT MAY COME as a surprise, but the appearance of dogs used to be considered less important than the ability to do a job. Through selective breeding, dogs were carefully matched for tendencies toward particular functions, such as herding, hunting or guarding. Dogs were bred for behavior to cement the desired traits. Today, all that has changed, and the majority of owners select their dogs on the basis of something other than the task for which they were bred, such as looks or prestige. In this chapter we will briefly review influences on your dog's ability and willingness to learn.

BREED CHARACTERISTICS

Breed characteristics can help or hinder your training, depending on what you want Cato to learn. Although breeding

objectives have changed over the years, the traits for which dogs were originally bred are still there to varying degrees. They influence the ease or difficulty of training, how readily the training will generalize and how often a learned behavior has to be reinforced.

Just because a dog has a hard time learning an exercise does not mean he is stupid. The **ease or difficulty** of training Cato is determined by the extent to which the task is in harmony with his instincts. For a retriever, learning to retrieve a dumbbell will be easy; for an Afghan, a little harder. A Sheltie will take to heeling more quickly than a Siberian Husky.

We often hear a dog labeled "stubborn" or "hardheaded." Using such terminology is called anthropomorphizing, that is, attributing human qualities to an animal. Abbey, the Beagle, for example, is high in prey drive, or hunting behaviors, for which the breed was developed. Her owner, Dan, wants to show Abbey in Obedience. Should Abbey catch the scent of a rabbit during the Heel Free and take off in hot pursuit, does that make her stubborn or hardheaded? Hardly! Our interpretation is that the exercise being taught is not in harmony with Abbey's instincts. She is a perfectly normal hunting dog, and Dan will have to work a little harder on suppressing her prey drive.

Have you ever said or heard someone say "Cato does fine at home, but when I take him out, forget it!" The strengths or weaknesses of Cato's instincts influence how quickly a learned behavior **generalizes** to new locations. Our Lab, Bean, is a natural retriever and quickly learned the Retrieve. Since retrieving is in harmony with his instincts, the behavior generalized itself easily to strange places, and he retrieves his dumbbell almost anywhere. Demi, our Dachshund, at first wanted nothing to do with a dumbbell and had to be taught to retrieve, step-by-step, over the course of several weeks.

In her case, the learned behavior did not easily generalize to new places. Although she would happily retrieve in the privacy and familiar surroundings of her yard, Demi did not think she could pick up the dumbbell in strange locations. It took several months of reviewing the teaching progressions for the Retrieve in different locations before Demi's response had generalized.

In Abbey's case, anytime she is taken to a new place, her

Instinctive behavior generalizes easily.

prey drive can kick in when she is off leash. Even though Dan may have taught her to respond perfectly to all the off-leash exercises in his backyard, he will have to start almost from the beginning and teach Abbey to respond in strange locations until Abbey's responses have become generalized.

Many handlers are under the impression that since the dog is now "advanced," this is no longer necessary. Quite the opposite is the case, and as the exercises become more difficult

Prey drive kicks into overdrive.

the need to train the dog in new and different locations increases. Training has not changed Cato's IQ. Anything new has to be taught the same way as the very first exercise—step-by-step.

Some exercises that to us appear as merely extensions of something the dog already knows can be dissimilar enough for the dog so that the previously learned responses do not generalize. Examples are the Front without a dumbbell and the front with a Dumbbell; Retrieving on the Flat and Retrieving over the High Jump; the Down at the side and the Drop on Recall; the Stays with the handler in sight and the Stays with the handler out of sight. These are just different enough that many dogs will have to be taught them almost as new exercises.

How often Cato will respond to a command before the response deteriorates is also dictated by breed characteristics. It is called the *principle of nonreinforced repetitions,* which says that the number of successive nonreinforced repetitions the dog will do depends on the extent to which the exercise is in harmony with its instincts. A nonreinforced repetition is the dog's response to a command or signal without any help from the handler—either reward or compulsion.

In Bean's case, once he has learned to retrieve, how many times will Bean fetch the dumbbell just on command? Although not forever, the number is easily more than twenty. For a Labrador, the exercise is self-reinforcing. How many times will an Afghan retrieve just on command? The one in our classes retrieved just twice in succession, which is enough to get a CDX leg.

For every exercise, the number of nonreinforced repetitions ranges from one or two to many, depending on the dog. The less instinctive the response, the fewer the successive nonreinforced repetitions the dog will do.

For example, the Utility go-out is an exercise which quickly breaks down, if not reinforced. After two or three go-outs, it is not unusual to see dogs not going out quite as far, not going quite as straight, not going quite as fast—the response getting poorer and poorer with each successive nonreinforced repetition. Parts of heeling, such as changes of pace and turns, in the case of most dogs, need to be reviewed often to maintain that crisp and enthusiastic response you want.

How do you know when you are about to run out of

nonreinforced repetitions? Cato will tell you, and as soon as you see the early signs, reinforce before his performance gets worse and you start to feel frustrated.

An understanding of this principle is important for those who wish to exhibit—you don't want to go into the ring having used up all your successive nonreinforced repetitions. Review and reinforce, if necessary, so that you can go into the ring with a clean slate. To reinforce a response we usually use the last teaching progression for the exercise.

TOUCH, SIGHT AND MENTAL SENSITIVITY

A dog's **touch sensitivity**, or threshold of physical discomfort, is another influence on learning. Use of a check is based on the theory of avoidance behavior. When Dan checks Abbey because her nose goes to the ground, she experiences discomfort which she will seek to avoid by keeping her nose off the ground. A dog with a high threshold of discomfort will require a stronger check than the dog with a low threshold. What may be an effective check in one case will barely be noticed in another. To complicate matters, Abbey's discomfort threshold increases in direct proportion with her interest in a given object or activity at the time. When Abbey comes across the scent of a rabbit, Dan's check will probably have to be considerably more emphatic to keep her focused on heeling than at other times.

Sight sensitivity, or the extent to which the dog is influenced by visual cues, also influences learning. Some breeds are more influenced by moving objects than others and require careful handling so that movements made by the owner do not lead to unintentional training. We have a Briard who is extremely sight sensitive—the slightest movement does not escape him. During heeling practice with D.J., we have to be careful to maintain an upright body posture and avoid any extra motions, because D.J. picks up everything. How he interprets what he sees can help or hinder the training.

Let's take the example of the check, which is often done by bringing the left elbow back and then forward, a motion that will be perceived by the dog. In many dogs this "pump" will produce anxiety because it telegraphs the check. Most dogs

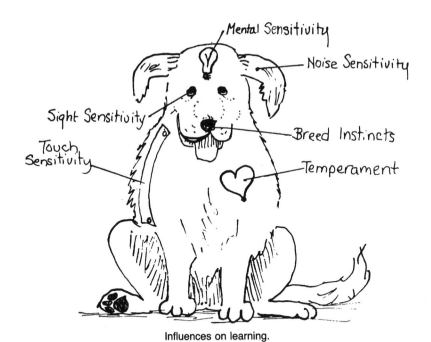

Influences on learning.

Touch sensitivity.

react by anticipating the check, that is, by tightening their neck muscles, thereby negating the effect. A simple rule is: The more motion involved in a check, the greater the adverse impact on the dog.

We recommend getting into the habit of checking without a pump of the elbow and limiting the movement of the arm to no more than four to six inches. If the arm moves more than that, there is either too much slack in the leash or the collar is too big for the dog.

A dog's **mental sensitivity** determines how it can deal with human emotions such as frustration, disappointment and anger. Coping abilities vary from dog to dog. For most, negative emotions in the handler cause confusion and anxiety in the dog, which impede learning and performance. The dog is unable to make the connection between its actions and the owner's feelings, as in "how could you do this to me?" When you get tempted to blame Cato, remind yourself who is in charge of the training program.

YOU AND YOUR DOG

Without any doubt, the most important influence on how Cato learns is your *attitude.* Bring a positive and benevolent attitude to training and Cato will be an eager and willing student. He will like the training and look forward to the daily sessions. Introduce him to each new exercise by showing what you want and he will try to learn. *Do not permit negative emotions,* whatever their source, to creep into your interaction with Cato.

Next time you take him out for a lesson, keep track of

Bring a positive and benevolent attitude toward training.

how many times you say "no," or use any other negative communications. Eliminate them altogether from your repertoire and concentrate on showing him in a positive way what you want him to do. Cato will reward you by learning quickly with willing responses.

During training, perhaps the most difficult situation for the trainer is the partially correct response. You give a command and Cato does something, but it is not quite what you had in mind. For example, you say "Heel," and he winds up in a crooked sit. He sat, but not straight. Your inclination is to reprimand Cato for the crooked sit—"he should know better." Alternatively, you give him a second command such as "sit straight." Neither is correct, although scolding him is more damaging to motivation than rewarding him.

The quickest way to destroy Cato's motivation is to reprimand him when he tries to obey a command, but falls short. Instead, don't say anything. Don't reprimand, don't give a second command and don't reward. *Start over* and show him what you want.

How many times you can repeat a particular maneuver or exercise, depends on Cato's Personality Profile. An exercise that is in harmony with his instincts, such as retrieving, you can repeat many times. An exercise that is not, stop after the first correct reponse. If you want to practice fronts or finishes, you can do fifty in row, should that be your inclination, provided you do them with or for him. When he does it on his own, stop after the first correct response, or he will become inventive. The correct response can be reinforced by praise or a treat.

The age at which Cato was separated from his canine family will have an effect on how he learns. The ideal time for Cato to leave the nest is at seven weeks of age, when he is neurologically complete and ready to bond to his new family.

A puppy separated from its mother and littermates significantly before seven weeks of age, as early as five weeks, may grow up developing an unhealthy attachment to its owner, which can result in overprotectiveness and aggression toward other dogs and people. It may also develop into a nervous and noisy dog. These behaviors may add to the level of difficulty of training such a dog.

Beginning with the fifth week, the puppies also learn basic

dog manners from their mother. She communicates to her puppies what is unacceptable behavior by low growls, snarls and, if necessary, snaps. The puppies learn what discipline is and to accept it. A puppy that has not had the benefit of its mother's instructions or interaction with its littermates, may resent discipline and respond with aggression to its owner's efforts to train it. Puppies learn that most important lesson of dog language—body postures and lip reading—so necessary for getting along with other dogs.

A puppy left with its mother or littermates much longer than the twelfth week, will grow up dog oriented. Bonding to humans may be difficult, if possible at all, as will be teaching the dog to accept responsibility for its own behavior. Such a dog may also be fearful of new situations.

Your dog's response to training will be influenced by its developmental and growth stages. For example, as Cato matures, he will undergo personality changes, some of which you will be able to observe. At first he may go through a phase where he is fearful of new situations. It is best not to make an issue out of this during training because it will pass all on its own. Once Cato is fully mature, he may buck for promotion and want to become the pack leader. That will not pass on its own and will interfere with your training unless you address it.

Getting Cato into shape is your job.

During growth stages Cato may experience physical discomfort and may not be able to sit squarely. When you observe this in your training, there is no point in insisting on a correct response until this growth stage has passed. The unspayed female's hormone changes may be difficult to handle. Behavioral changes do vary from female to female, as does the length of time between seasons, and you will want to find out how your female reacts during these times so that you can assess the impact on your training.

You also have to consider Cato's physical condition and overall health. Advanced training is similar to an athletic undertaking and you want to make sure Cato is in shape. It will be difficult to convince a fat dog that jumping is a barrel of laughs. Should Cato refuse to do something he previously did willingly and without difficulty, it may be due to a physical problem.

Your dog's muscle structure dictates your warm-up, which is what you should do before you even start a season. A dog with round, heavy muscles needs at least twice as long to stretch and loosen up than a dog with elongated, light muscles.

One comment we hear frequently is that Cato loves Open, but hates Utility. Compare what Cato has to do in Open with

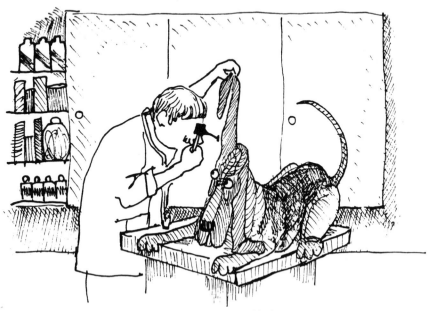

Overall good health is critical.

what he has to do in Utility in terms of the inherent nature of each exercise. We characterize exercises by how our dogs perceive them, as either motivating (action) or demotivating (control). The Utility exercises require more control from the dog's point of view, than do those required for Open as seen in the following chart.

Exercise	Action	Control
OPEN		
Measuring		X
Heeling	X	
Drop on Recall		X
Retrieve	X	
High Jump	X	
Broad Jump	X	
UTILITY		
Measuring		X
Signal Exercise		XXX
Scent Discrimination		X
Directed Retrieve	X	
Moving Stand		X
Directed Jumping	XX	

In the Open class, except for the Stays, there are only two control exercises, one of them measuring. Is it any wonder that dogs love this class? They get to have fun with retrieving and jumping.

In Utility the exact opposite is true; out of six, only two are action exercises. Moreover, the Signal Exercise calls for the Stand, the Down and the Sit, which out of all the Obedience maneuvers have the most depressing and demotivating effect on Cato. Aren't dogs supposed to have any fun in Utility?

Did you know that over the years, Utility has been the most frequently and extensively revised Obedience class? Could this reflect a continuous dissatisfaction with Utility because of the demotivating nature of the exercises?

Once you recognize how Cato perceives what you are teaching, you can then make the necessary adjustments to maintain his enthusiasm. For example, how many times in a row should you practice the Signal Exercise if it is obvious that it negatively affects Cato's motivation? Once, is the answer, then do something else he likes, such as a retrieve, and then try it again. Observe Cato's reaction to training so you can help him where he needs motivation.

Prey drive.

Pack drive.

Fight

Flight

Defense drive.

30

3

The Concept of Drives

There is no domestic animal which has so radically al-
tered its whole way of living, indeed its whole sphere
of interests, that has become domestic in so true a
sense as the dog.

Konrad Lorenz

INSTINCTIVE BEHAVIORS, those our dogs have inherited from their ancestors and that are useful to us in the training process, can be grouped into three categories—**prey, pack** and **defense**—collectively called drives. Each one of these is governed by a basic trait.

Every dog is an individual who comes into the world with a specific grouping of genetically inherited, predetermined behaviors. How those behaviors are arranged, their intensity and how many component parts of each drive the dog has will determine temperament, personality, suitability for the task required and how the dog perceives the world.

BEHAVIORS IN EACH DRIVE

Prey drive encompasses those inherited behaviors associated with hunting, killing prey and feeding. It is activated by motion, sound and smell. Behaviors associated with prey drive are seeing, hearing, scenting, tracking, stalking, chasing, pouncing, high-pitched barking, jumping up, biting, killing, pulling down, shaking, tearing and ripping apart, carrying, eating, digging and burying.

You see these behaviors when your dog is chasing a cat or when Katharina gets excited and barks in a high-pitched tone of voice as the cat runs up a tree. Katharina may also shake and rip apart soft toys and bury her dog biscuits in the couch.

Pack drive groups together behaviors associated with being part of a pack, including reproduction. Our dogs are social animals who evolved from the wolf. To hunt prey mostly larger than themselves, wolves have to live in a pack, which means adhering to a social hierarchy governed by strict rules of behavior to assure order. An ability to be part of a group and to fit in is important, and translates itself into a willingness to work with man as part of a team.

Pack drive is stimulated by rank order in the social hierarchy. Physical contact, playing and behaviors associated with social interaction with another dog—reading body language— as well as reproductive behaviors—such as licking, mounting, washing ears and all courting gestures—are part of pack drive. The ability to breed and to be a good parent are also part of pack drive.

A dog with many of these behaviors is the one that follows you around the house, is happiest when with you, loves to be petted and groomed and likes to work with you. The dog may be unhappy when left alone, which can express itself in separation anxiety.

Defense drive is governed by survival and self-preservation, and consists of both fight and flight behaviors. It is more complex because the same stimulus that can make a dog aggressive (fight), can also elicit avoidance (flight) behaviors, especially in the young dog.

Fight behaviors tend not to be fully developed until the dog is over two years of age, although tendencies toward these behaviors will be seen at an earlier age. It can be observed in Bully, the dog that "stands tall," stares at other dogs and likes to "strut his stuff." Bully will stand his ground or go toward unfamiliar things, guard his food, toys or territory from other

32

dogs or people and may dislike being petted or groomed. Bully is the one that will lie in front of doorways or cupboards, and his owner walks around Bully because he won't move on his own. These are all defense drive (fight) behaviors.

Flight behaviors demonstrate that the dog is unsure. Hackles that go up the full length of the body, hiding or running away from a new situation, a dislike of being touched by strangers or a general lack of confidence are all flight behaviors. Freezing (not going forward or backward) can be interpreted as inhibited flight behavior.

PERSONALITY PROFILE FOR DOGS

To help us understand how to approach each individual dog's training, we cataloged twelve behaviors in each drive that influence the dog's responses useful to us in training and created the Personality Profile. The twelve behaviors chosen are those that most closely represent the strengths of the dog in each of the drives. The Profile does not pretend to include all behaviors seen in a dog nor the complexity of their interaction.

The results of the Profile will give you a good starting point for tailoring a training program to your dog's needs. You can then make use of Konrad's strengths, avoid needless confusion and greatly reduce the time it takes him to learn.

When completing the Profile, keep in mind that it was devised for a house dog or pet with an enriched environment, including some training, and *not* for a dog kept solely in a kennel. A kennel dog has fewer opportunities to express as many behaviors as a house dog. Answers should indicate those behaviors Katharina would exhibit if she had not been trained to do otherwise. For example, did she jump on people or the counter to steal food before she was trained not to do so? Other behaviors are, in turn, only seen in a training context, for example, during distraction training.

The fight part of the defense drive does not fully express itself until the dog is mature, around two to four years of age, depending on the breed, although tendencies toward those behaviors may be seen earlier. Young dogs tend to exhibit more flight behaviors than older dogs.

Personality Profile for _____

Prey Drive

Does your dog   YES   NO
 1. Sniff the ground or air a lot?   ☐   ☐
 2. Get excited by moving objects, for example, kids on ☐   ☐
    bikes or squirrels?
 3. Stalk cats, others dogs or objects in the grass?   ☐   ☐
 4. When excited, bark in a high-pitched voice?   ☐   ☐
 5. Pounce on toys or the dumbbell?   ☐   ☐
 6. Jump on the kitchen counter to steal food?   ☐   ☐
 7. Shake and "kill" toys?   ☐   ☐
 8. Rip soft objects apart?   ☐   ☐
 9. Wolf down food?   ☐   ☐
10. Like to carry things?   ☐   ☐
11. Like to dig?   ☐   ☐
12. Bury things?   ☐   ☐

Pack Drive

Does your dog   YES   NO
 1. Get along with other dogs?   ☐   ☐
 2. Get along with people?   ☐   ☐
 3. Bark when left alone?   ☐   ☐
 4. Solicit petting or like to snuggle with you?   ☐   ☐
 5. Respond to verbal praise?   ☐   ☐
 6. Like to be groomed?   ☐   ☐
 7. Seek eye contact with you?   ☐   ☐
 8. Tremble or whine on stays?   ☐   ☐
 9. Act like your shadow and follow you around?   ☐   ☐
10. Play a lot with you or other dogs?   ☐   ☐
11. Jump up to greet people?   ☐   ☐
12. Show a lot of reproductive behaviors, for example, court- ☐ ☐
    ing or mounting another dog?

Defense Drive (Fight)

Does your dog YES NO
1. Stand his ground or go toward and investigate strange objects or sounds? ☐ ☐
2. Like to play tug-of-war games to win? ☐ ☐
3. Bark or growl in a deep tone? ☐ ☐
4. Guard his territory? ☐ ☐
5. Guard his owner(s)? ☐ ☐
6. Guard food or toys? ☐ ☐
7. Dislike being petted? ☐ ☐
8. Dislike being groomed or bathed? ☐ ☐
9. Growl or bite the leash when checked? ☐ ☐
10. Dominate other dogs with neck hackles up and ears forward? ☐ ☐
11. Like to fight? ☐ ☐
12. Get picked on by older dogs (if a young dog)? ☐ ☐

Defense Drive (Flight)

Does your dog YES NO
1. Run away from new situations? ☐ ☐
2. Hide behind you when he can't cope? ☐ ☐
3. In distraction training, trying to avoid the distractor by going in front of or behind you? ☐ ☐
4. Run away on Stay exercises? ☐ ☐
5. Crowd during heeling? ☐ ☐
6. Put all hackles up when meeting a new person or dog? ☐ ☐
7. Have difficulty coming close to you on the Recall or Retrieve exercises? ☐ ☐
8. Crawl on belly or turn upside down when verbally reprimanded? ☐ ☐
9. Have difficulty standing still on Stand Stay when examined by a stranger? ☐ ☐
10. Submissively urinate when he thinks he has made a "mistake"? ☐ ☐
11. Submissively urinate during greeting behavior? ☐ ☐
12. Show a tendency to bite when cornered? ☐ ☐

Prey Drive	Yes _____	No _____
Pack Drive	Yes _____	No _____
Defense (Fight)	Yes _____	No _____
Defense (Flight)	Yes _____	No _____

Now what?

Before you can use the results of the Profile, you first have to take a look at what you are trying to teach Konrad and which drive he has to be in to perform a given exercise correctly.

In Novice, Konrad has to learn to Heel On Lead, Stand for Examination, Heel Off Lead, come when called and do a Sit and Down Stay. All of these exercises require him to be in pack drive. All else being equal, a dog with many pack behaviors (more than six) should have no trouble with this routine.

In Open, Konrad has to be measured, Heel Off Lead, Come—Drop—Come, Retrieve on the Flat, Retrieve over the High Jump, do a Broad Jump and a Sit and Down Stay with the handler out of sight. Now it gets a bit more complicated and *in addition* to *pack drive* behaviors, we need *prey drive* behaviors for the retrieving and jumping exercises.

In Utility, Konrad has to be measured again (it seems we still don't know how tall he is), do the Signal Exercise, Scent Discrimination, Directed Retrieve, Stand from Motion, and Directed Jumping, another *mix* of *Pack* and *Prey drive* exercises.

Theoretically, dogs do not need **defense drive** (fight) behaviors for Obedience exercises, but the absence of these behaviors has important ramifications. It is pivotal and determines how the dog has to be trained.

The beauty of the drives theory, if used correctly, is that it gives us a tool to overcome a dog's "weaknesses." For example, it can be used to teach a dog with few prey behaviors how to retrieve and a dog with few pack behaviors how to heel.

Defense drive (fight)—its importance

One of our dogs, a lovely Lab named Bean, had what we considered a curious problem, curious since none of our other dogs displayed this behavior. His worst exercise was the Recall. In addition to anticipating the command, he would come with head and tail down, body arched, taking tiny short steps. Then he would stand about six feet in front of the handler and slowly and gingerly sit, looking miserable throughout the entire exercise. To us, this was not acceptable since our idea of the Recall is a dog who comes briskly and joyously, with ears forward and tail wagging.

Looking at Bean's Profile and analyzing the drive he has to be in for the Recall gave us the answer to how he had to be trained. Bean's main weakness—if you want to call it that—is that in Defense (fight) he scored only 2, and in Defense (flight), 6. He scored 9 in Prey and 9 in Pack.

When I would leave Bean, a hand signal was used as well as a voice command to "Stay." Since he had a tendency to anticipate, both were emphatic, with my left shoulder dropping, if ever so slightly, as I gave the signal. Quite unintentionally, I was putting him into Defense drive, his weakest suite, for an exercise requiring him to be in Pack drive. Since he had only two behaviors in Defense (fight), he became stressed and was unable to cope, which reflected itself in anticipation and hesitant Recalls.

After becoming aware of what was happening, I first eliminated the "Stay" signal altogether. Before leaving him, I lightly touched him on top of the head. Then I made a special effort to stand absolutely straight, smiling at him as I told him to "Stay" in a light tone of voice. I would walk away—the same fifty feet—turn, pause, but now lean backward as far as I could without falling over, with my weight on my heels, and as I called, raise my hands upward from the side. It was incredible; not only did he stay until he was called, but he bounded to me, screeched to a halt right in front with a straight

Bean was taught the recall using prey drive.

sit, head up, ears forward and tail wagging! My idea of a recall, and we knew we were on the right track.

For Bean it meant he no longer was in Defense Drive where he has very few coping behaviors. I had put him there by using a deep tone of voice and a strong Stay signal.

By touching him on top of the head, eliminating the signal and using a lighter tone of voice, I left him in Pack drive, where he had to be in the first place. When I called, by using a higher pitched tone of voice, leaning backward, plus the movement of my hands, I put him into Prey drive where he loved to be and where he was comfortable. After he had sat in front, I could put my hands at my side, straighten out my body and praise him, thereby putting him into Pack drive where he eventually needed to be.

The key is knowing which drive Konrad has to be in for any given exercise, and, if he is in the wrong drive, how to switch him into the correct one. One example is the handler's body posture:

1. leaning toward or over Konrad, puts him into Defense drive
2. standing up straight with a relaxed body posture and benign facial expression puts him into Pack drive
3. leaning backward or running away from him, puts Konrad into Prey drive

Quick
Motions
↑
Hand signals —

Toys — ⊘

COME!

High pitched tone
of voice

— Food

— leaning
backwards

(also running away
from the dog).

Praising
|
GOOD!

Eliciting prey drive.

BRINGING OUT DRIVES

Now that you can visually recognize which drive Konrad is in when you are working, you need to know how to keep him in the correct drive.

Here are the basic rules:

1. **Prey** drive is elicited by the use of hand signals—motion—(except stay), a high-pitched tone of voice or an object of attraction—stick, ball or food—chasing or being chased and leaning backward with your body.
2. **Pack** drive is elicited by touching, praising and smiling at the dog. Grooming, playing and working with him with your body erect, all bring out pack drive behaviors.
3. **Defense** drive behavior is elicited by leaning over the dog, either from the front or the side, checking, a harsh tone of voice and use of the Stay hand signal.

erect body posture —

— smiling

— Petting (also grooming and working the dog)

Eliciting pack drive.

SWITCHING DRIVES

Konrad can instantaneously switch himself from one drive to another. Picture him playing with a favorite toy (Prey), when the doorbell rings. He drops the toy and starts to bark (Defense). You open the door and it is a neighbor whom Konrad knows. He goes to greet the visitor (Pack) and returns to play with the toy (Prey).

Harsh tone of voice

STAY!

leaning over the dog

checking with the leash

use of stay signal

Eliciting defense drive.

Our task was to figure out how to switch the dog from one drive into another. For example, I am teaching Katharina to Heel on Leash in the yard when a rabbit pops out of the hedge. She spots it, runs to the end of the leash, straining and barking excitedly in a high-pitched voice. She is in full bloom Prey drive. How do I get her out of Prey into Pack where she needs to be in order to Heel? If I check or verbally reprimand her, I put her in Defense when I really want her in Pack. The answer is that to get a dog out of Prey and into Pack, you must first teach the dog to go through Defense, at least until the dog has learned to do it herself.

Since Katharina has a large number of Defense (fight) behaviors, I gave her a check, which switched her out of Prey into Defense. To get her back into Pack, I touched her gently on the top of her head, smiled at her and told her how clever she was. Then we continued to work on heeling. In Bean's case, a check would have been too much, and an "ah, ah" sufficient to put him out of Prey into Defense.

When Konrad is in Defense and we want him to be in Pack drive, we still have to use Defense drive. The use of a check, or a stern tone of voice and leaning over the dog, are effective for the dog with a large number of Defense (fight) behaviors.

For the dog that has few *fight* behaviors and a large number of *flight* behaviors, the use of the leash is counterproductive. Use of the body, that is, bending over the dog, or a deep tone of voice, are usually enough to elicit Defense drive. For example, if Bean jumps on the counter to steal food, a verbal reprimand, not much more than clearing my throat, is sufficient to switch him out of Prey into Defense (flight). During training, if I use the leash to check Bean, his reaction (or overreaction) is extreme. He goes upside down, his body is rigid and can hardly move.

Here are the basic rules for switching:

1. From **Prey** into **Pack** in the teaching process, you go through Defense. Once Konrad has learned what you want him to know, he switches himself. How you put your dog into Defense will depend on the number of defense (fight) behaviors he has, for example, check, voice, body posture. As the dog learns, the need to go

through Defense drive from Prey into Pack becomes less and less, and voice or a slight change in body posture will suffice.

2. from **Defense** into **Pack** by touching or smiling.
3. from **Pack** into **Prey** with an object (food) or motion.

Applying the concept of drives and learning which drive Konrad should be in and how to get him there, will speed up your training process enormously. You will no longer confuse Konrad. As you become aware of the impact your body stance and motions have on the drive your dog is in, your messages will be perfectly clear to your dog. Your body language is in harmony with your expectations. Since Konrad is an astute observer of body motions (this is how dogs communicate with each other), Konrad will understand exactly what you want.

Example of body posture contradicting words said.

PRACTICAL APPLICATION

By looking at your dog's profile, you will know which training techniques work best and which are in harmoy with your dog's drives. You now have the tools to tailor your training program for your dog.

Defense (fight)—more than six yes responses in the Profile and fewer than six defense (flight). Your dog will not be bothered too much by compulsion.

Body posture is not critical, although contradictory postures on your part will slow down the training. Tone of voice should be firm but pleasant and nonthreatening.

Defense (flight)—more than six yes responses in the profile and fewer than five defense (fight). Your dog will not respond to compulsive training, and you will have to rely mainly on the other drives.

Correct body posture and quiet, pleasant tone of voice are critical. *Avoid* using a harsh tone of voice and any hovering, leaning over or toward your dog. There is a premium on positive, congruent body postures and gentle handling.

Prey—more than six yes reponses in the Profile. Your dog will respond well to use of an Object of Attraction (OA) during the teaching phase. May need strong compulsion, depending on strength of Defense drive (fight), to suppress Prey drive when in high gear, such as when chasing a cat or spotting a squirrel. Easily motivated, but also easily distracted by motion or moving objects.

Signals will mean more to this dog than commands. Premium on using body, hands and leash correctly so as not to confuse the dog.

Prey—fewer than six yes responses. Your dog is probably not easily motivated by food or other objects, but is also not easily distracted by moving objects.

Pack—more than six yes responses. Responds readily to praise and touch. Your dog likes to be with you and will respond with little guidance.

Pack—fewer than six yes responses. Start praying. Mary probably does not care whether she is with you or not. She likes to do her own thing and is not easily motivated. Your only hope is to rely on prey drive in training. Usually breed specific for dogs bred to work independently of people.

By now you have gathered that the easiest dogs are those that are balanced among all drives. No matter what you do, the dog seems to be able to figure out what you want. If you are lucky enough to have a dog like Katharina, take good care of her. By applying the principles of drives, she will do well by you.

Dogs that exhibit an overabundance in Prey or Pack are also easily trained, but you will have to pay more attention to the strengths of their drives and exploit those behaviors most useful to you in training. Now you have the tools to do it!

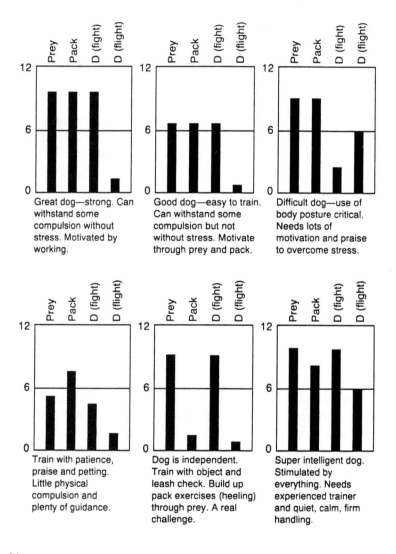

Great dog—strong. Can withstand some compulsion without stress. Motivated by working.

Good dog—easy to train. Can withstand some compulsion but not without stress. Motivate through prey and pack.

Difficult dog—use of body posture critical. Needs lots of motivation and praise to overcome stress.

Train with patience, praise and petting. Little physical compulsion and plenty of guidance.

Dog is independent. Train with object and leash check. Build up pack exercises (heeling) through prey. A real challenge.

Super intelligent dog. Stimulated by everything. Needs experienced trainer and quiet, calm, firm handling.

4

Stress and Your Dog

Stress has long been the subject of physiological and psychological speculation.

Herbert Benson

STRESS IS DEFINED as the body's response to any physical or mental demand. The response prepares the body to either fight or flee. It increases blood pressure, heart rate, breathing and metabolism, and there is a marked increase in the blood supply to the arms and legs. It is a physiological, genetically predetermined response over which the individual, be it a dog or person, has no control.

When stressed, the body becomes chemically unbalanced. To deal with this imbalance the body releases chemicals into the bloodstream in an attempt to rebalance itself. The reserve of these chemicals is limited. You can dip into it only so many times before it runs dry and the body loses its ability to rebalance. Prolonged periods of imbalance result in neurotic behavior and the inability to function.

"Bear is a happy and enthusiastic worker until I take him to a Trial. Then he is slower than molasses in January. All his get up and go seems to have gone and went. What can I do to

45

motivate him?" We get this question more than any other in our seminars and training camps. We believe the answer relates to stress and Bear's ability to deal with it.

Mental or physical stress ranges from tolerable all the way to intolerable—that is, to the inability to function. Our interest here deals with stress experienced during training, whether we are teaching a new exercise or practicing a familiar one, or during exhibiting. We want you to be able to recognize the signs of stress and what you can do to reduce the stress your dog may experience. Only then can you prevent stress from adversely affecting your dog's performance.

POSITIVE AND NEGATIVE STRESS— MANIFESTATIONS

Stress is characterized as "positive" when it manifests itself in **in**creased activity and "negative" when it manifests itself in **de**creased activity. Picture yourself returning home after a hard day at work. You are welcomed by a mess on the brand-new white living room carpet. What is your response? Do you explode, scream at poor Bear, your spouse, the children and then storm through the house slamming doors? Or do you look at the mess in horror, shake your head in resignation, feel drained of energy, ignore the dog, the spouse and the children and retire to your room?

In the first example, your body was energized by the chemicals released into the bloodstream. In the second example, your body was debilitated.

Dogs react in a similar manner, and stress triggers the fight/flight response. Positive stress manifests itself in hyperactivity, such as running around, bouncing up and down or jumping on the handler, whining, barking, mouthing, forging or anticipating commands. You may think your dog is just being silly and tiresome, but for the dog those are coping strategies. Negative stress manifests itself by lethargy, such as freezing, lagging and a slow response to a command. Your dog lies down under your chair at a match or show and goes into a deep sleep, or at training class wants to stay in a corner of the room and not participate. Far from being relaxed, those are the coping behaviors for negative stress. Another example is the dog that

46

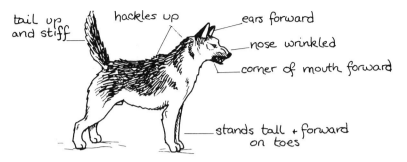

tail up and stiff

hackles up

ears forward

nose wrinkled

corner of mouth forward

stands tall + forward on toes

Stress triggers the fight . . . or flight response.

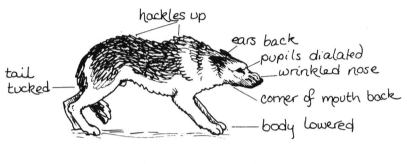

hackles up

ears back

pupils dialated

wrinkled nose

corner of mouth back

body lowered

tail tucked

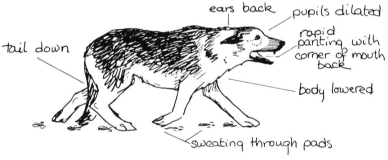

tail down

ears back

pupils dilated

rapid panting with corner of mouth back

body lowered

sweating through pads

Signs of stress.

slowly goes to the scent articles, takes a long time to make a decision and crawls back to the handler.

Signs of either form of stress are muscle tremors, excessive panting or drooling, sweaty feet that leave tracks on mats, dilated pupils, in extreme cases urination or defecation—usually in the form of diarrhea—and self-mutilation. Behaviors, such as crowding or going in front of or behind the handler during distraction training are stress related, as are anticipation or not leaving the handler's side.

47

Stress is a normal part of our lives, and it is the little "stresses" that go on every day that adds to the wear and tear on the body, the mess on the rug being the last straw. It becomes the threshold beyond which you can no longer concentrate or function normally, and you then become anxious.

Anxiety

Anxiety is a state of apprehension, uneasiness. When it is prolonged two things happen. First the ability to learn and to think clearly is diminished and ultimately stops. It can also cause a panic attack. Second, anxiety depresses the immune system, thereby increasing our chances of becoming physically ill. It affects our dogs in the same way. The weakest link in the chain is attacked first. If the dog has structural flaws, such as weak pasterns, the animal may begin to limp or show signs of pain. Digestive upsets are another common response to stress.

Stress, in and of itself, is not bad or undesirable. A certain level of stress is vital for the development and healthy functioning of the body and its immune system. It is only when there is no behavioral outlet for stress—for example, when the dog is put in a no-win situation—that the burden of coping is borne by the body and the immune system starts to break down.

SOURCES OF STRESS—INTRINSIC AND EXTRINSIC

Sources of stress are either intrinsic or extrinsic. **Intrinsic** sources are all the things that come with the dog, including structure and health. Intrinsic sources are inherited and come from within the dog. Dogs vary in coping abilities and stress thresholds, and what you see is what you get. Realistically, there is not much you can do to change your dog, such as "train" it to deal better with stress. You can use stress-management techniques to change the impact of stress.

Extrinsic sources range from the diet you feed to the relationship you have with your dog. Extrinsic sources come from outside the dog and are introduced externally. They include lack of adequate socialization, appropriateness of the training method being used, the location where the training takes place,

48

Stress creates anxiety.

frustration and indecision on your part and how the dog perceives the environment. Fortunately, all these are under your control.

STRESS AND LEARNING

All learning is stressful. For many, ourselves included, one of the most recent learning experiences was brought on by the computer revolution. In our case, there were plenty of times during the learning process when we were tempted to throw the stupid contraption out the window. At that moment, learning and the ability to think rationally stopped. There was no point in trying to go on until the body had the chance to rebalance itself.

When you train Bear, you cannot prevent him from experiencing stress, but you can keep the stress at a level where he can still learn. Recognize the signs of stress and know when you should stop. When Bear reaches the point where he can no longer learn, whatever he does will be the result of random, redirected or displacement behaviors and will not be committed

49

Poor diet stresses the system.

to memory. Even though he may do the exercise, his anxiety level will be such that he will not learn or retain anything under those circumstances.

There are going to be times when Bear just doesn't get the message. It can happen during the teaching phase or the practicing phase, especially when you are working with distractions. Nothing you do works, and you feel you are not making any progress.

"What can I do?" we are often asked. "If I stop, Bear will think he has won and he will never do it for me." This argument is completely without any merit because it presupposes that you and Bear are adversaries in some kind of a contest, as in, "you will do it no matter what." *It is not a question of winning, but of teaching Bear.* You can walk away from a training session at any time, whether or not you think you have been successful. When you see that no further learning is taking place, stop! If you don't and insist on forcing the issue, you will undermine your dog's trust in you and undermine the relationship you are trying to build.

Give Bear a rest for several hours and try again, and all of a sudden the light bulb will seem to go on. By having taken a break at that point, you gave latent learning—the process of absorbing knowledge over time—a chance to work.

Our advice is to quit training when you find yourself becoming irritable or when Bear starts to show signs of severe stress.

Konrad Most, the "father" of training as we know it today, recognized the importance of maintaining the dog's equilibrium. In his 1910 training manual he wrote, "Good training needs a kind heart as well as a cool and well-informed head. . . ." Anyone can dominate a dog by physical or mental pressure, but only through the building of confidence through positive reinforcement can a reliable performance take place. Bear must perceive you as trustworthy or he will begin to exhibit neurotic behavior.

Avoid training techniques that needlessly stress your dog.

STRESS AT SHOWS

When Mary took Bear to their first match they were not as well prepared as she had thought. Mary was extremely nervous as she went through their routine, and Bear was distracted by all the other dogs. They did not do well, and as they came out of the ring Mary was embarrassed and frustrated. "How could you do this to me" she scolded Bear, who immediately became apprehensive and anxious. For him, this was not a good first experience. From then on, he exhibited signs of significant stress at dog shows.

First impressions have the most lasting impact, so it is important that Bear's first experience at a match or show be a pleasant and enjoyable one. We recommend to our students that they take their dogs to a match just to visit and get their dogs accustomed to such events before entering an obedience class. As an alternative, we suggest that they enter in a con-formation class at a match or show where they can give their dog treats in the ring, talk to them and just have fun. In either case, *the object is to make it a positive experience for the dog.*

Through your training, expose Bear to different situations so that he learns to cope with new experiences and environ-ments and is not overwhelmed by new surroundings.

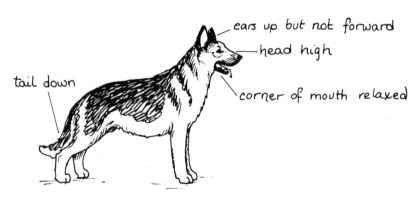

ears up but not forward
head high
corner of mouth relaxed
tail down

Relaxed body posture.

STRESS MANAGEMENT

Become aware of *how* Bear reacts to stress, that is positively or negatively, and the *circumstances* under which he shows signs of stress. It could be a location or something you are doing. Your goal is to restore Bear's breathing pattern and body posture to normal.

Let's say Bear reacts to stress in a positive way, which means he gets overexcited and bouncy. In the case of a person we would say he or she is hysterical. In the old movies, when someone started screaming uncontrollably, this was handled by slapping the person on the cheek. For Bear, a check on the collar to settle him down would be the same thing. Keep your hands still and off your dog, with your voice quiet, or you will excite him even more. Give him the down command and enforce it. If he is in a crate, take him out and give him some exercise. Every behavior has a time frame, and experience will tell you how long it takes Bear to calm down under different circumstances. During times of severe stress, Bear is unable to learn or perform, and you must have his body balanced as soon as you can to avoid unnecessary wear and tear on his immune system.

If Bear reacts to stress in a negative way, use a walk to get the circulation going and redistribute the chemicals that have been released, so his breathing can return to normal. At a show, massage the top of his shoulders to relax him; just because he is quiet does not mean he is calm. Warm him up with an object or food. Under no circumstances try compulsion to get him "out of it." It will produce even greater lethargy.

Understand that *Bear has no control over his response to stress—he inherited this behavior—*and that it is your job to manage it as best as you can. With every successful repetition through proper management, Bear will become accustomed to going to shows and handle them like an old trooper.

YOU AND STRESS

How do you manage the manifestations of stress you experience at shows? Did you ever notice that the same exercises are a lot harder when going for legs than when you already have your title? It is your responsibility to prepare yourself and your dog. Realize how your feelings affect your dog, and that managing his stress is just as important as managing your own. We teach our students to concentrate on their dogs' physical comfort and mental outlook, to count while heeling, and to work on their own breathing—anything to get them to think about something other than their own feelings. It's difficult to get nervous when you have a job that requires your full attention.

Next comes the warm-up, which requires you to concentrate on getting Bear ready to go into the ring. Using the drives theory and what you have practiced during training, you have carefully thought out the program that you now must follow. And before you know it, you're in the ring and you can't get nervous even if you wanted to because you have to count to maintain your pace, concentrate on turns and changes of pace and keeping Bear at just the right level of animation. If you do all that, there is no time to become anxious, and you will have done your part to help Bear.

Should Bear not qualify in one or more of the exercises, it is your job to make sure that does not affect his performance for the remainder of the routine. Our test for handler composure and stress management is the scores for the exercises after the dog has failed.

PART II

Open Training

5

Heeling

---

*The principle feature of this exercise is the ability of
the dog and handler to work as a team.*

AKC Obedience Regulations

WE RECOGNIZE that your dog already knows
how to Heel, and if the two of you consistently score 40 points
on this exercise you can skip this chapter. If not, look at it as
a brief refresher course on motivation. You may even find a
helpful hint or two that will improve your understanding of
heeling and your scores.

UNDERSTANDING HEELING

Heeling is deceptive—it looks easy when done well. Because
of its seeming simplicity, in the beginning some trainers don't
take it very seriously and may ignore it altogether once they
are past Novice.

In reality, it is the most complex of all the Obedience
exercises. Next time you are at a Trial, make it a point to look
at the judge's score sheet posted at the Superintendent's or

Trial Secretary's table after the class is finished. You will notice that heeling is the one exercise in the Novice class where a good share of the exhibitors will have lost more points than on all the other exercises combined. Since it is the only exercise where we work directly with our dog, it does not take a genius to figure out who is at fault.

The Obedience regulations define "Heel position" as the "area from the dog's head to shoulder shall be in line with handler's left hip." The area from head to shoulder will vary, depending on the size of the dog, from less than four inches to do more than eighteen inches. The handler's "left hip" also leaves room for variation. We recommend that for Heel position you pick a point in the center of the "area from the dog's head to shoulder" to be in line with the seam of your trousers.

The Regulations further require that in any position "the dog shall be straight in line with the direction in which the handler is facing, at the handler's left side, and as close as practicable to the handler's left leg without crowding, permitting the handler freedom of motion at all times." (AKC Reg., Chapter 2, Section 18.)

When your dog falls behind Heel position, it is lagging; when ahead of Heel position, it is forging. When your dog interferes with your freedom of motion or bumps you, it is crowding; when your dog gets away from your left side, it is

Establishing Heel position.

heeling wide. And at all times your dog's entire body, including the rear end, has to be straight in line with the direction you are facing. Your dog may already Heel perfectly or may need help in some areas.

Once you have figured out where Buddy should be while heeling, train him to maintain that position at all such times without lagging, going wide, forging or crowding. How much variation should you accept? That's entirely up to you and how many points you are willing to give up so long as you remember that Buddy will take this exercise only as seriously as you do.

Start paying attention to those areas where Buddy needs help (see Practicing Heeling, p. 63). For example, when you change pace from slow to normal, what does Buddy do? Does he stay in heel position, or does he lag or go wide or both? You have to keep your eye on him during heeling so you can tell.

Many dogs have a tendency to lag and/or to go wide when the handler accelerates (the start, slow to normal, normal to fast) or makes turns away from the dog (right and about turns). Conversely, dogs tend to forge and/or crowd when the handler decelerates (halt, normal to slow, fast to normal) or makes a turn into the dog (left turn). Now that you know what Buddy is likely to do, it becomes second nature to anticipate his response and help him to do it correctly.

HEELING AIDS

When teaching our dogs to Heel and remain in Heel position, we use a number of aids, such as our body language, pace and footwork.

Let's take a look at **body language,** consisting of posture and movements. Dogs communicate with each other through body language. Whether or not we are aware of it, we, too, use our bodies to communicate with our dogs. To avoid confusing them as to what we want, our body language must be consistent, that is, not in conflict with other actions. We cannot, for example, turn the upper part of our body and look back at the dog while at the same time checking Buddy forward to speed him up. The two actions are incongruent—one tells Buddy to stay back (turning our upper body to look), the other to speed up (check forward). The net result is a confused, uncertain and anxious Buddy, and because he is not responding correctly, a frustrated handler. Without any doubt, the greatest impediment to successful heeling is the handler's incongruent body posture. If you don't believe us, have someone videotape your heeling and look at what you do with the upper part of your body and how your dog responds.

For heeling, we want to communicate to the dog "remain in Heel position," which we do by keeping the body upright, shoulders square, facing forward. In teaching our dogs to accelerate, we lean forward; to decelerate, we straighten up. Turning any part of our body toward the dog or dropping the left shoulder says to the dog "hang back." It is useful when we want the dog to slow down (left turn, inside turn of figure eight), but incorrect any other time.

You will have to decide what to do with your arms while heeling. Fortunately, you do not have much choice. The regulations require either that "the handler's arms and hands shall *move* naturally at the handler's sides while in motion . . . or the right hand and arm *must* move naturally, while the left hand shall be held against, and centered in front of the body, in the area of the waist." (AKC Reg., Chapter 2, Section 19, emphasis ours.) So you only have two choices; naturally swing both arms as you walk, or put the left hand against your belt buckle and swing the right. As a general rule, we recommend keeping the left hand at your waist. Any exceptions would be based on your dog's Profile and how it is trained. For example, a dog strong in Prey but weak in Defense (fight) drives, would benefit from having the left hand move at the side. You *cannot* clutch your trouser leg with either hand or keep the right hand still.

Your **pace** is another aid in heeling. Make it consistent, and pick one that is comfortable for you and makes Buddy look his best. If you have trouble maintaining the same pace, use music, count or buy a $15 pocket metronome from a music store. If your pace is too slow, your dog will lag; if it is too fast, you look ridiculous. The regulations require you to walk "briskly and in a natural manner," which has nothing to do with speed as such. We interpret it as alert and energetic. For the fast, the handler must run and the dog must noticeably accelerate in speed. We suggest that the handler maintain the same length of stride but at least double the normal speed. For the slow, we suggest the handler maintain the same length of stride, but reduce speed by at least one half. Each change of pace should be pronounced so there is a definite and discernible (by the judge) difference.

Finally, there is **footwork,** which consists of keeping your feet together, pointing them in the right direction and not slowing down or tripping in the process. We recommend that footwork be practiced without the dog until it becomes second nature.

Start—you can start with either leg, as long as you are consistent. Our own preference is to start on the right leg. It is one less thing to worry about, seems to work better for our dogs than starting on the left and is more comfortable for us. It is also the leadoff leg for all further footwork. You may want to experiment with what works best for you and your dog.

Halt—shorten the length of your stride as you come to a halt, but maintain the same speed. You can stop on your right foot and bring up the left, or you can stop on the left and bring up the right. It will not matter to your dog as long as you do it the same way each and every time.

Right Turn—stop on your right foot, plant the left pointed in the direction of the turn (instep of left foot to toe of right) and step into the turn on the right. Maintain the same rhythm or your dog will lag. *Hint:* Keep counting.

Left turn—stop on your right foot, plant the left pointed in the direction of the turn (heel of left to instep of right) and step into the turn on the right. *Hint:* Keep counting.

About Turn—stop on your right foot, plant the left pointed in the direction of the turn (instep of left to toe of right, same as for the right turn), bring around the right, bring around the left and place it one foot length in front of the right and step out on the right. Do not step back on your right or slow down. *Hint:* Keep counting.

Changes of Pace—when you change pace, make your leadoff leg the same as for the start and push off on the opposite leg.

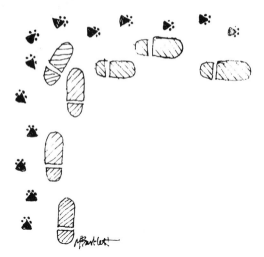

Diagram of the right turn.

Diagram of the left turn.

On top of all these maneuvers, you will have to learn to walk a straight line, perhaps the most difficult part of heeling, and learn to come to a halt and make an about turn without stepping into your dog. *Hint:* Try walking the way you do without your dog, normally, with your head up instead of looking at the ground.

Control position.

PRACTICING HEELING

To maintain our dogs' motivation, we use three techniques: the release, an object and if necessary a check.

Release—A simple, yet effective way to teach your dog to accelerate and to relieve stress. With your dog sitting at Heel, hold the leash in control position (CP), no more than one-half inch of slack, both hands on the leash, comfortably below your waist. Say "OK," or pick your own release word, move out at a trot, stepping off on your leadoff leg, five steps forward, then tell him what a good puppy he is (there is no sit). Be enthusiastic and get him excited about moving with you. Use the release for the start, coming out of turns and changes of pace. Exaggerate the movement of the leadoff leg to give Buddy the idea it signifies acceleration.

Object—Hold your object in your right hand at your right side, the leash neatly folded in the left with no more than one-half inch of slack. As the leadoff leg moves, bring your right hand in front of your dog's nose and give him the object. By controlling the position of the object, you keep your dog in the exact position you want him to be.

Check, if necessary—Use a check where you would use the object and then give him the object. Let's say Buddy, who responds to being checked (profile), still lags when going from slow to normal after you have worked with the release and the object. Check straight forward in the direction you want him to go as you change pace on the leadoff leg and before Buddy falls behind, then give him the object and praise.

After you have used a check, try again without a check. If you see Buddy try, praise or reward in accordance with his profile. *What you do when he tries will influence his motivation more than anything else.*

Any time you use a check, always do so in the direction you want the dog to go. If you do not, you engage in unintentional training, the most common example being the automatic sit at heel. The handler checks diagonally across his body and the dog sits crooked. Buddy has to, because the check made him do it. Crowding, too, is taught through the incorrect use of the leash, checking into the handler. For turns watch your left shoulder and be sure you and Buddy are facing in the new direction before you check.

Continue to review distraction training with Buddy just as you did in Novice. We prefer slow to normal pace when heeling past the distractor because Buddy will have to concentrate that much harder on not being distracted. If he goes by the distractor without being distracted, praise and release. If he becomes distracted and looks at the distractor, check upward toward your face. Praise when he looks at you, then release.

Use the distractor for the Start, Changes of Pace and the Right and About Turns. We do this in class, with the students helping as distractors for each other's dogs. Remember, the purpose of distraction training is to build Buddy's confidence and ability to concentrate.

How close you can get to the distractor depends on your dog's profile and training experience. We start this exercise by heeling the dog past the distractor from about two feet away, with each pass gradually bringing Bean closer and closer, until Bean almost touches the distractor as he goes by. If your dog tries to push you away from the distractor or rushes ahead of you or tries to go behind you, you are too close to the distractor.

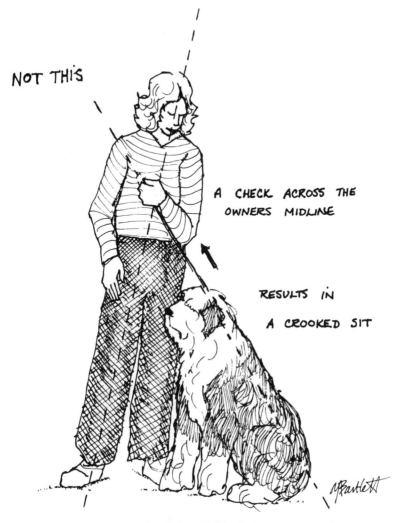

NOT THIS

A CHECK ACROSS THE OWNERS MIDLINE

RESULTS IN

A CROOKED SIT

Incorrect use of leash.

You need to build Bean's confidence before getting quite so close.

One of the most common complaints we hear is "My dog does fine on leash, but when I take the leash off he [take your pick] sniffs—lags—runs away—doesn't pay attention—is distracted." If this sounds like you, review Buddy's heeling on leash around distractions, paying particular attention to responses at potential trouble spots. For example, how are the starts, changes of pace from slow to normal and normal to fast,

Heeling with distractor two feet away.

Getting closer to the distractor.

and the right and about turns? Your dog will tell you where he needs help and in what form, whether it be release, object or check.

With Strings Attached

Concentrate on maintaining the same pace and body posture when Buddy is off leash, or you will confuse him. You may want to incorporate heeling with a kind of umbilical cord in your sessions on a regular basis. It gives you the feel of off-leash heeling with Buddy still on leash. It also teaches you how to reinforce off-leash heeling and Buddy to accept the reinforcement.

Heeling with the umbilical cord looks like this:

- With Buddy sitting at Heel, take the loop end of the leash in your right hand and pass it around your back to your left hand.
- Take the snap and thread it through the loop.
- Tighten the leash around your waist so that the *loop* is in Heel position.
- Attach the leash to the collar.
- Put your left hand where you normally hold it for off-leash heeling and start.

Anytime Buddy deviates from Heel position, *slowly* reach for and put two fingers of your left hand through the collar at the side of his neck. Back to front and palm facing you, bring him back to Heel position, guiding him by the collar. Let go of the collar and tell him what a clever puppy he is.

When you reach for Buddy, be sure you do it slowly and deliberately. If you try to grab for him, you will cause him to become afraid of your left hand and shy away from it, which makes the technique useless. Taking hold of the leash negates

Setting up . . .   for the umbilical cord.

the purpose of this approach, which is to teach you how to reinforce a command when Buddy is off leash (as in no leash) and for him to accept that reinforcement. Once you move your left hand, you must follow through. Don't threaten to reinforce and then just wave your left hand somewhere in the vicinity of the collar.

Practice heeling with the umbilical cord until you are comfortable with the technique, and Buddy can successfully navigate past distractors. Then practice changes of pace. Next, unsnap the leash from the collar and put the bolt in your pocket, leaving a little of the leash dangling at your side. That is the final step in the transition from on-leash heeling. If Buddy still deviates from heel position, reinforce the same way as you did for heeling with umbilical cord. Keep in mind that you are now practicing testing and that 90 percent of your time should be spent in the practicing phase, on leash, control position.

FIGURE EIGHT

Even though Buddy already knows how to do the Figure Eight, you still have to practice and make sure he can do it off leash. The Figure Eight is another heeling exercise and the same principles and progressions apply, as well as the same heeling aids—body language, pace and footwork.

Body language on the Figure Eight means giving your dog the right cues at the right time. For the inside turn your dog must slow down, and for the outside turn speed up in order to remain in Heel position, while your pace remains the same. You already know how to achieve both just by the direction in which you turn your left shoulder.

In addition to pace, which has to be the same as for your other heeling, you must pay attention to position in relation to the "posts." We suggest that you stay about an arm's length away from the posts and that you maintain that position throughout the entire exercise. It is not uncommon to see handlers winding up two or even three arm's lengths away from the post after the inside turn (could this be Buddy getting in your way?), and then almost crash into the right shoulder of the post for the outside turn. To avoid these mistakes, you may want to chart your course without your dog so you get the feel of where *you* are supposed to be in relation to the posts. *Hint:* Keep your head up. It is difficult to maintain the same distance from the posts when you are looking at the ground.

Our footwork for the Figure Eight consists of pointing each foot in the direction of the post as we go around. Our leadoff leg for the inside turn is the right. When you point the right toward the post, it will cause the upper part of your body to rotate slightly back, telling your dog to slow down. The opposite happens on the outside turn where your leadoff leg is the left. The Figure Eight footwork also needs to be practiced without your dog. *Hint:* Start the Figure Eight by going to the left—the most common way. You don't want to wake up the judge and make him think.

You will have to experiment where to make the switch for the leadoff leg. For most dogs, the switch leads to best results when it is made one step past the post. If your dog needs motivation use the release, your object or a check where he needs it.

If you are going to use the check, be careful about direction. We do not recommend checking Buddy as he is rounding a turn because it fails to give him a clear direction. If Buddy lags on the outside turn, use a check as you make the switch to the leadoff leg coming out of the inside turn. If he goes wide at the end of the outside turn, check lightly toward you when you are parallel with the post and before you make the switch to the leadoff leg for the inside turn.

For the foundation of heeling and more information, see *Teaching Dog Obedience Classes: The Manual for Instructors.*

CONCLUSION

So much for simplicity. It sounds a great deal more complicated than it really is, and you are probably using similar techniques already but have not had them explained quite this way. You may have a dog that is able to compensate for your shortcomings in handlings and make you look good no matter what you do. If so, so much the better. On the other hand, you may have an "average" dog that needs all the help it can get, in

6

Drop on Recall

The principal features of this exercise . . . are the dog's prompt response to the handler's command or signal to drop, and the dog's remaining in the Down position until again called or signaled to Come.

AKC Reg., Chapter 4, Section 6.

Y OU MAY not be aware of the visual cues you are giving your dog. To make sure you are not inadvertently moving some part of your body—even as much as a finger—have someone watch you or stand in front of a mirror and watch yourself.

SEQUENCE 1.
REVIEW RESPONSE TO DOWN COMMAND, DOG SITTING AT HEEL

From her Novice work, Pinky is already familiar with the "Down" command. Test her understanding. With Pinky sitting at Heel and without giving her any visual cues (such as pointing to the ground, bobbing your head, leaning over or bending

71

your knees) quietly say "Down." If she lies down, praise, count to five and release.

If she does not respond to the command or her response is unacceptable, such as not prompt enough, slowly slide your left hand down the leash all the way to the snap and "check" straight down. Keep your elbow locked and your arm at your side. Avoid checking across your body as that will teach Pinky to curl in front of you. Stand up, praise and release. Repeat until your dog lies down on command at your side. Sequence 1 is the *reinforcement* progression.

When you are trying to decide what is an unacceptable response, keep in mind that your dog's size and structure determine how it performs this exercise. Some dogs are structurally unable to lie down without first going into the sitting position. Others can only lie on one side or the other, but not square, which will influence the speed of the second come.

Down at side, handler stops.

SEQUENCE 2.
DOWN AT SIDE FROM MOTION, HANDLER STOPS

With Pinky sitting at Heel, say "let's go" and start to walk. *The command "Heel" is not used because this is not a heeling exercise.* After several steps, say "Down" *as* you come to a halt. If you stop and then say "Down," Pinky may confuse the exercise with the automatic sit.

Praise when she does it and then release straight forward. The release here is the beginning of teaching Pinky to move briskly forward from the Down position.

If she does not drop, slowly slide the left hand down the leash to the snap and check straight down, praise and release. Count to five between your praise and the release.

SEQUENCE 3.
DOWN AT SIDE FROM MOTION, HANDLER CONTINUES

Before you try sequence 3, review 1 and 2. Say "let's go" and after having walked for several steps, say "Down" and continue

Down at side from motion, handler continues on to the end of the leash.

Handler releases backward.

walking to the end of the leash, turn to face Pinky, praise, count to five and release backward. When you release her, remember you are teaching her to come briskly to you after you have dropped her.

If Pinky does not drop, start again, and as you give the command slowly slide your left hand down the leash to the snap and check straight down, then go to the end of the leash, turn, praise, pause and release. When she responds reliably, go on to the next progression.

SEQUENCE 4.
DROP FROM FAST, HANDLER CONTINUES

Before you try sequence 4, review 1 and 3. Now visualize how your dog comes to you on a recall. It is at that speed that she will have to drop on command and *without* any unnecessary steps. While you may not be able to run as quickly as she can, teach her to drop from a fast pace as you continue to the end of the leash.

SEQUENCE 5.
STOP AND DROP FROM IN FRONT

When Pinky has mastered the drop from fast, you are ready to try the exercise with her coming toward you.

- Leave her on a Sit Stay and go to the end of the leash, facing her.
- Call with "Come" and as she comes to you, take a step toward her on your right foot, keeping the left foot in place.
- Signal by bringing your right arm straight up and say "Down."
- Keep the upper part of your body straight.

Stepping toward Pinky will cause her to stop her forward progress.

After she has dropped, bring the right foot back, lower your arm, praise, count to five and release. Use the release backward to teach her to come again quickly and enthusiastically after you have dropped her. If Pinky does not drop, review sequence 1 with a check and sequence 4, then try it again. Even if she lies down on command at your side, reinforce with a check as she drops. The check reminds Pinky what she has to do.

Stop and drop from in front.

75

A word of caution: Once Pinky is coming toward you, do *not* check her into a down, or do anything else she may perceive as unpleasant because it will adversely effect her recall. *What is important here is your dog's view of what is unpleasant and not yours!* If she needs help, work on the exercise from heel position and *not* when she is coming to you.

SEQUENCE 6.
STOP AND DROP FROM IN FRONT, OFF LEASH

Repeat sequence 5 off leash. You may want to review sequence 1 with a check before you try this. As Pinky responds, gradually increase the distance between you and her.

Maintain the "step, command and signal" sequence until she is reliable. After that, first eliminate the step, and then decide whether you prefer voice or signal. You will probably want her to respond to either.

SEQUENCE 7.
DISTRACTIONS

Begin by having a distractor crouch about two feet from Pinky's line of travel and where you intend to drop her. Call and give her the command or signal to drop.

She may do one of several things, such as anticipate the drop, drop after she has gone past the distractor, not drop at all, avoid the distractor by arcing away from him, not respond to the come command or actually do it correctly—not likely the first time you try this. What Pinky is telling you is that she lacks the confidence to drop near the distractor, and it is your job to show her that she can do it. Her confidence will increase with each successive correct repetition.

If Pinky anticipates, slowly go to her without saying anything, put the leash on the dead ring of the collar and with a little tension on the collar show her exactly what she should have done by guiding her backward to the spot where you called. Have Pinky sit in front, praise and release backward. No extra command is given. Should Pinky still antici-

Drop with distractor nearby.

pate after several repetitions, put the leash on the live ring of the collar and use a check to show her what she is supposed to do.

If Pinky drops past the distractor or does not drop at all, slowly approach her without saying anything, put two fingers of your left hand, palm facing you, through the collar, back to front, at the side of her neck, take her to the spot where she should have dropped and reinforce the command from in front. The command is *not* repeated. Return to the spot where you originally gave the command, praise your dog, count to five and enthusiastically release.

If Pinky arcs away from the distractor or does not respond to the come command, slowly approach her without saying anything, put the leash on the dead ring of the collar and with a little tension on the collar show her exactly what you wanted her to do, such as guiding her past the distractor. For arcing away from the distractor, use two distractors, facing each other about eight feet apart, and teach Pinky to drop between the distractors.

Pinky may also start to anticipate the come from the down, in which case you slowly approach your dog without saying anything, put two fingers of your left hand, palm facing you, through the collar, back to front, at the side of her neck, take her back to the spot where she should have stayed and reinforce the down from in front. Do not repeat the command. Turn around and return to the spot where you originally gave the command, praise your dog, count to five and enthusiastically release.

As Pinky gains confidence and responds correctly, work your way through the different levels of distractions. Since you have already trained her to ignore these distractions for the Novice recall, it will not take her very long to figure out what you want.

SIGNAL OR COMMAND

Experiment with Pinky to decide whether you should use a signal or a command when in the ring. Pinky's Profile should help you with your decision. If she is weak in Defense (fight) drive, you will be better off using the command rather than the signal.

7

The Retrieve

The principal feature of this exercise is that the dog re-trieve promptly.

AKC Reg., Chapter 4, Section 8.

THERE ARE three basic approaches to teaching the Retrieve—food, force and hope. Of the three, the least reliable is the last. We are not suggesting that a dog trained with the hope method, also called play retrieve, cannot get Obedience titles. We have a Yorkshire Terrier, Ty, who was never taught the Retrieve. When Ty was six months old, he did Scent Discrimination with articles made for our Landseer Newfoundlands, literally staggering under the weight. Ty is a compulsive retriever, and if he could carry it back, he would— be it a dumbbell, a scent article or a glove.

What we are suggesting is that Dingo at some point— usually when it counts—*may* refuse to Retrieve. An easy way to find out is to practice the distraction training described in this chapter. If he passes, you probably have little to worry about. If he does not, consider going through the teaching progressions. For the dog that already retrieves, it will be like a review and go quickly. When you are finished, you will have a Retrieve you can reinforce.

The Motivational Retrieve, although it relies mainly on reward, is a combination method. Its goal is to produce a happy, confident and reliable retriever, using the groundwork described here.

SEQUENCE 1.
EQUIPMENT NEEDED

Enthusiastic handler, dumbbell, small can of cat food and metal spoon. Start teaching this exercise when Dingo is hungry, such as before meals.

SEQUENCE 2.
WORD ASSOCIATION

- Place food, spoon and dumbbell on a chair.
- With your dog sitting at Heel, say "take it" and give him a small portion of food with the spoon.
- Repeat ten times or until Dingo readily opens his mouth to get the food.

2. Word association. Since Diggy is a small dog, we do this on a table.

SEQUENCE 3.
PUTTING THE DUMBBELL IN THE DOG'S MOUTH

- Place your left index finger behind his left canine tooth and gently open his mouth.

3. Opening Diggy's mouth . . . (notice the cat food)

and putting the dumbbell in.

Cup mouth shut.

- With your right hand place the dumbbell in his mouth.
- Rest the thumb of your right hand on top of his muzzle, fingers under his chin, and cup his mouth shut.
- **Praise** enthusiastically.
- Say "give" and take the dumbbell out of his mouth.
- Reward with food.

Repeat fifty times over the course of several sessions, or after rest periods between every ten repetitions.

SEQUENCE 4.
DOG TAKES THE DUMBBELL VOLUNTARILY

- Put two fingers of your left hand through the collar, back to front, palm facing you, at the side of the dog's neck.
- Offer the dumbbell with "take it" while touching the small whiskers in front of his mouth with the bar.
- If he takes it, briefly cup mouth shut, **praise**, remove and reward with food.
- If he does not take it, watch for signs of intention behavior, such as licking, nosing dumbbell, or intensely staring at it.

When you see *intention* behavior, take your hand out of the collar, open his mouth, put dumbbell in and briefly cup mouth shut. **Praise**, remove and reward with food. Repeat until Dingo readily opens his mouth and accepts the dumbbell. It is important that you praise while he has the dumbbell in his mouth—that is the lesson—and not after you have taken it out.

SEQUENCE 5.
HOLDING THE DUMBBELL

- Put the dumbbell into Dingo's mouth and say "hold it."
- Make a fist with your right hand and hold it under his chin.
- **Smile**.

4. Put two fingers of your left hand through the collar . . .

and offer the dumbbell by touching the small whiskers in front of his mouth.

83

- If Dingo starts mouthing the dumbbell or looks as though he is going to open his mouth to drop the dumb-bell, give him a gentle chuck under the chin with "hold it."
- **Praise**, remove and reward with food.

Repeat twenty times over several sessions and gradually increase time of hold to thirty seconds.

SEQUENCE 6.
REACHING FOR THE DUMBBELL

- Put two fingers of your left hand through the collar at the side of the dog's neck, back to front, palm facing you.
- Present dumbbell two inches in front of his mouth with "take it."
- If he does, cup mouth shut with "hold it."
- **Praise**, remove and reward.

5. Holding the dumbbell.

If he does not:

- *Lightly* twist the collar by rotating your left hand a quarter of a turn toward you, which will bring his head forward and toward the dumbbell, until he reaches for and takes it.
- Cup mouth shut with "hold it."
- **Praise**, remove and reward.

Do not twist the collar for more than thirty seconds or try to increase pressure more than a quarter of a turn. Instead, put the dumbbell in his mouth, cup shut with "hold it," **praise**, remove and reward. Repeat until Dingo voluntarily reaches for and takes the dumbbell.

SEQUENCE 7.
WALKING WHILE HOLDING THE DUMBBELL

- Put the dumbbell in your dog's mouth with "take it."
- Say "hold it" and encourage him to walk two steps forward.
- Put your right hand under his chin when he starts to move to give Dingo confidence.
- **Praise**, remove and reward.
- Repeat until Dingo is successful, then gradually increase number of steps to twenty.

SEQUENCE 8.
TAKING THE DUMBBELL WHILE MOVING

- Say "let's go."
- With your dog in motion, present the dumbbell with "take it" at mouth level.
- In two-inch increments, and with your dog in motion, gradually lower the dumbbell to the ground.
- Keep your right hand on the dumbbell until Dingo takes it.
- **Praise**, remove and reward.

8. Taking the dumbbell while moving.

Should Dingo become stressed during this sequence, the following will happen:

1. If he is a negative stressor, he will clamp his mouth shut when you apply pressure on the collar, turning inward, twisting lightly. Pressure on the collar will not make him open his mouth. Stop applying pressure on the collar, put the dumbbell in Dingo's mouth, praise, reward and try again.
2. If he reacts to stress positively, he will engage in re-directed behaviors, one of which will be to grab the dumbbell, at which point you **praise**, remove and re-ward.

SEQUENCE 9.
PICKING UP THE DUMBBELL FROM THE GROUND

- With fingers through the collar, place the dumbbell on the ground.
- Keeping your right hand on it, say "take it."
- When Dingo picks up the dumbbell, say "hold it," and back up two steps.
- **Praise**, remove and reward.

9. Picking up the dumbbell from the ground.

Then:

- Still with your fingers through the collar, place the dumbbell on the ground and hold your right hand one inch away.
- Say "take it, hold it."
- Back up two steps.
- **Praise**, remove and reward.
- Gradually hold your right hand first two inches, then six inches and then twelve inches away from the dumbbell.

If Dingo does not pick up the dumbbell, *lightly* twist the collar until he picks it up. Should this sequence become an issue and Dingo continues to refuse to take the dumbbell, review the prior progressions. Be sure you followed them religiously and that your dog has mastered each one before you went on to the next one.

Finally, say "Stay," and place the dumbbell one foot in front of Dingo. Return to your dog and send him with "take it." **Praise**, remove and reward. Repeat by first placing it three feet and then six feet in front of your dog.

SEQUENCE 10.
THROWING THE DUMBBELL

- Throw the dumbbell a few feet and at the same time send Dingo with "take it."
- As soon as he picks up, call him.
- **Praise**, remove and reward.
- Gradually increase the distance the dumbbell is thrown.
- As he gains confidence, first eliminate the recall command, and then introduce the sit in front with "hold it."
- **Praise**, remove and reward.

SEQUENCE 11.
RING ROUTINE

- Put two fingers of your left hand through Dingo's collar, say "Stay" and throw the dumbbell.
- Very, very gingerly let go of the collar.
- Count to five and say "take it."
- **Praise**, remove and reward.
- Repeat until your dog holds the Stay without having to hold him by the collar.

If at any time he needs motivation, throw the dumbbell while *at the same time* saying "take it," letting him chase after it. **Praise**, remove and reward.

SEQUENCE 12.
DISTRACTIONS

Now that Dingo knows how to Retrieve, he is ready for distraction training. During distraction training, you will see the following responses or variations thereof:

1. Dingo starts going toward the dumbbell, but then backs off and fails to retrieve, meaning "I don't have the confidence to get close enough to the distractor to retrieve my dumbbell."
Remedy: Without saying anything, **slowly** approach him,

11. Ring routine.

put two fingers of your left hand through the collar, back to front, palm facing you, at the side of his neck and take him to the dumbbell. If Dingo picks up the dumbbell, praise and release; if he does not, put the dumbbell in his mouth, praise and release. **The command is** *not* **repeated**.

Try again. You may find that you have to help Dingo several times before he has the confidence to do it by himself. Once he has done it on his own, *stop!*

2. Dingo leaves altogether and does not Retrieve, saying in effect "I can't cope with this."
Remedy: Same as in 1.

3. Dingo does nothing, meaning "if I don't do anything maybe all of this will go away."

Remedy: Same as in 1.

4. Dingo permits himself to be distracted or takes the dumbbell to the distractor.

Remedy: Same as in 1, except if he takes the dumbbell to the distractor, **slowly** approach your dog without saying anything, put the leash on the dead ring of the training collar and, with a little tension on the collar, show him exactly what he was supposed to do by guiding him to you. **No extra command is given**.

5. Dingo anticipates the Retrieve, meaning he is catching on and wants to show you how clever he is.

Remedy: Without saying anything, **slowly** approach, take the dumbbell out of his mouth, put it down where he picked it up, go back to the starting point and then send him. Whatever you do, don't shout "no," or do anything else that would discourage retrieving after you have just worked so hard to get him to pick up the dumbbell.

6. Dingo does it correctly and that is when you stop for the session.

Introduce Dingo to distractions as follows: The distractor stands about two feet from the dumbbell and assumes a friendly posture, not threatening to the dog. Send Dingo. As soon as he picks up the dumbbell, **enthusiastically release**. Look at the exercise as having been completed as soon as Dingo picked up his dumbbell. As he gains confidence, the distractor stands a little closer, and then over the dumbbell.

The distractor also hides the dumbbell by standing directly in front of it with his back to the dog, and then lightly puts a foot on it. You can use a chair as a distraction by putting the dumbbell under the chair and then on the chair.

Continue to use food rewards for Dingo on a random basis, that is, not every time but often enough to maintain motivation.

When Dingo confidently retrieves under these circumstances, introduce second degree distractions. The distractor crouches close to the dumbbell and tries to distract him by saying "here puppy, puppy." The distractor does *not* use your dog's name.

Once Dingo has successfuly worked his way through that level, third degree distractions are added, such as offering the dog food or a ball or toy. Of course, the distractor never lets the dog have the food.

Distractions add an extra dimension and take training to a higher level. Distraction training builds your dog's confidence and teaches him to concentrate on what he is doing. It is especially important for a shy dog to gain the confidence it needs to respond correctly under differnt conditions.

During distraction training, keep in mind that any time you change the complexity of the exercise, *it becomes a new exercise for the dog.* If Dingo goes for the food, you would treat that response the same way you did when you first introduced distraction training. No, Dingo is not defiant, stubborn or stupid, just confused as to what he should do and has to be helped again.

JUST HAVING FUN

By challenging Dingo to use his head, you can increase the strength of the responses and increase his confidence in the ability to perform under almost all conditions.

A word of **caution**: While distraction training is exciting and fun, use common sense. If after several tries Dingo is not successful and becomes anxious about the exercise, stop. Ask yourself, "Does he have to do this in order to get a qualifying score?" If the answer is no, don't make an issue out of it! In the ring, chances are your dog will have an easy retrieve with no immediate distractions.

When using distraction training, it is also important to give Dingo a chance to work it out for himself. Don't be too quick to try and help. Be patient and let him try to figure out independently how to do it correctly. Once that happens, you will be pleasantly surprised by the intensity and reliability with which he responds.

1. Introduce dog to jump.

2. On leash, dog jumps.

92

8

Retrieve Over the High Jump and the Broad Jump

THE HIGH JUMP

> *The principal features of this exercise are that the dog go out over the jump, pick up the dumbbell and promptly return with it over the jump.*
>
> AKC Reg., Chapter 4, Section 10

Sequence 1. Introduce the dog to the high jump

- Put your leash on the dead ring of Demi's training collar.
- Walk her up to the jump.
- Set the jump at teaching height—the dog's height at the elbow.
- Touch the top board and let her examine the jump.

Sequence 2. On the leash, the dog jumps

- Start from ten feet, facing the jump which is where she will eventually sit when you send her.

- Say "Demi, jump" and walk briskly toward the jump, letting her go over.
- Don't run—you want Demi to be able to focus on the jump.
- Either go over the jump with her or go around it.
- **Praise** as she lands on the other side.
- Repeat until Demi is comfortable going over the jump.

To avoid future jumping problems, let Demi find her own style and *do not* try to *force* her over the jump by pulling on the leash. Should she lack the confidence to go over the jump, encourage her with a treat or lift her over once or twice so that she sees it can be done. Repeat five to ten times per session. Jumping repetitions are not only necessary to teach Demi the exercise, but also to condition her physically. Make this your warm-up progression every time you work on this exercise.

Sequence 3. Dog jumps by herself and from different angles

- Leave Demi ten feet from the jump and go to the other side by stepping over the jump.
- Focus her attention on the center of the top board.
- Take three steps backward, pause and say "Demi, jump." It is not a good idea to tap the top board as you say "jump," because it teaches your dog to jump on a visual cue instead of the command.
- Once you see that she has committed herself to jump, back up to give her enough room to land.
- **Praise** as she lands and release backward.

Few of us can throw the dumbbell so that it always lands in the right spot, and some of us never get it there. So you might as well teach your dog to jump from different angles. Leave Demi facing the right upright of the jump, ten feet away, go to the other side by stepping over the jump, focus her attention on the center of the top board, take three steps backward, pause and say "Demi, jump."

Repeat by leaving your dog facing the left upright part of the jump. Then leave her one foot to the right (left) of the right (left) upright, focus her attention on the jump, step back, pause and say "jump."

94

3. Focus dog's attention on the center of the jump.

3. Dog jumps by herself.

95

Sequence 4. Dog jumps while holding the dumbbell

Repeat sequence 3 with Demi holding her dumbbell as she jumps.

Sequence 5. Motivational Retrieve

- With Demi at heel, put two fingers of your left hand, palm facing you, through your dog's collar at the side of her neck, back to front.
- Hold the dumbbell in your right hand and get her excited about retrieving the dumbbell.
- From ten feet away from the jump, say "Demi, jump" and briskly approach the jump.
- Two feet before you get to the jump, throw the dumbbell and let go of your dog.
- You continue to approach the jump, and as she takes the jump, picks up the dumbbell and turns around to look at you, focus her attention on the center of the jump.

4. Dog jumps while holding the dumbbell.

- As she commits herself to jump, back up to give her enough room to land.
- **Praise**, take the dumbbell and release.
- Repeat until your dog jumps, retrieves and returns reliably.

Once the dog has confidence, practice this sequence with "bad" throws so your dog learns to come back over the jump from different angles. Picture a forty-five degree line from each upright and condition Demi to return over the jump from anywhere within that area.

Sequence 6. Sending her from a stationary position

- From ten feet away from the jump, tell Demi to stay and put two fingers of your left hand through her collar.
- Throw the dumbbell.
- Very, very gingerly let go of the collar, count to five.
- Say "Demi, jump."

After she has jumped, quietly follow her and, after she has picked up the dumbbell and turned to face you, focus her attention on the center of the jump. As she commits herself to return, back up so she has enough room to land, take the dumbbell and release. Repeat until she stays without two fingers in the collar and returns without any help from you. Position yourself facing the center of the jump at least eight feet away and throw the dumbbell at least eight feet beyond the jump.

Practice "bad" throws as in sequence 6.

Sequence 7. Raising the jump height

- Begin raising the jump in two- or four-inch increments, depending on the size of your dog.
- If the height of the jump becomes an issue, condition your dog at a lower height.
- Difficulties with jumping are never disciplinary in nature: Your dog is trying to tell you something. Listen to her!

7. Raising the jump height.

Sequence 8. Distractions

- Follow the program outlined in Chapter 5.
- In addition, have a distractor stand close to an upright while the dog is jumping. Once she is successful, have the distractor try to get your dog to go around the jump on the return by talking to her or enticing her with food.

Any time your dog goes around the jump on the return, slowly approach your dog, put two fingers of your left hand, palm facing you, through the collar at the side of her neck, back to front, take her back to where she picked up the dumb-bell, tell her to stay—she can stand, sit or lie down—go to the other side of the jump, focus her attention on the top board, step back and tell her "jump." **Praise** as she lands and release. Then try it again.

Demi may also try to go around the jump on the way out, in which case you slowly approach her and, if she has picked up the dumbbell already, take it out of her mouth and put it back where she picked it up. Now return with Demi to the starting point and send her again.

98

8. Adding distractions.

If she fails to retrieve altogether, and you are sure it is *not* a jumping problem, follow the procedure described in Chapter 5.

In a testing situation, make it easy for your dog to center on the jump for the return by throwing the dumbbell a little off center so that when she turns to come back she is facing the center of the jump. Most dogs turn consistently either to the right or the left for the return.

BROAD JUMP

The principal features of this exercise are that the dog stay where left until directed to jump and that the dog clear the jump on a single command or signal.
AKC Reg., Chapter 4, Section 12

Sequence 1. Introduce your dog to the jump

- Use two boards *and* the bar jump (with uprights) in between, set at teaching height—the height of the dog at the elbows.
- Put the leash on the dead ring of the collar.
- Walk Demi up to the jump and let her examine it.

99

1. Introduce dog to the Broad Jump.

Sequence 2. On leash, dog jumps

- From ten feet away from the jump, say "Demi, over" and walk briskly toward the jump, letting the dog jump.
- You can jump with her or go around it.
- **Praise** as she lands.
- Repeat until your dog is comfortable going over the jump.

Repeat five times per session to condition your dog, and make this your warm-up progression every time you work on this exercise. To save time, it is perfectly permissible to go in either direction.

Sequence 3. Dog jumps by herself

- Leave your dog ten feet away from and facing the jump.
- Go to the other side, preferably by stepping over the jump.
- Focus her attention on the center of the bar, take three steps backward, pause and say "Demi, over."
- When you see that she has committed herself to jump, back up.
- **Praise** as she lands and release.
- Repeat five times per session.

2. On leash, dog jumps.

3. Focus dog's attention on center of the bar.

101

Sequence 4. Introduce fence

To help your dog understand what is expected from her, make an extension of the Broad Jump with a ten-foot section of fencing.

- Focus Demi's attention on the center of the bar.
- Stand at a right angle to the end of the fence.
- Send her with "Demi, over," at the same time signaling with your right arm *and* right leg.
- Say "Come" as she lands, turn to your right and back up three steps.
- **Praise** and release.

As your dog gains confidence, begin increasing the length of the jump by adding, if necessary, one board, and, if she has to jump four, one more, keeping the bar in the center as nearly as you can. Once she jumps the full distance reliably, start positioning yourself to your left, in two-foot increments, until you can stand midway between the boards.

Sequence 5. Eliminating the uprights

Remove the uprights from the bar jump, reduce distance to teaching width and place the bar on the first board of the broad jump. Then follow the steps as in sequence 4.

Sequence 6. Eliminating the fence

Remove the fence and place the bar in its place. Review the steps as in sequence 4. When Demi reliably makes the turn to come to you, eliminate the "Come" command.

Sequence 7. Distractions

- Have the distractor positioned about two feet from where Demi is going to land.
- Over the course of several sessions, work your way through first, second and third degree distractions.
- If she goes to the distractor, slowly and without saying anything go to her and put the leash on the dead ring of the collar.

4. Introduce fence.

4. Standing opposite the jump.

103

5. Eliminating the uprights.

7. Adding distractions.

104

- With a *little* tension on the collar show her exactly what you wanted her to do.
- Then try it again.

You can also test her understanding of the exercise by leaving her with her back to the jump before sending her, or on a down facing the jump and on a down with her back to the jump. If Demi refuses to jump or goes around it—not likely at this stage—slowly and without saying anything, go to her, put the leash in the dead ring of her collar and review Sequence 2 five times, and start all over.

In practice, we leave the bar in position at all times to keep Demi jumping straight. It is removed during a test, for one repetition. Should Demi jump at an angle toward you, repeat, but this time, after she has started to approach the jump and before she has taken off, place your right leg between the two center boards so that she will jump straight.

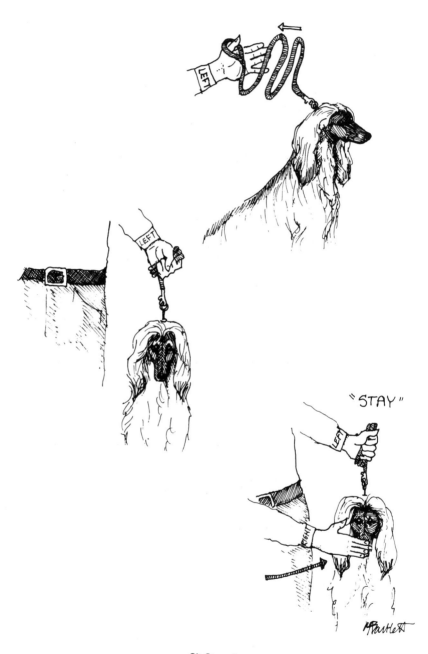

"STAY"

Sit Stay, 1.

9

The Stays—
Sit and Down

The principal feature of these exercises is that the dog remain in the sitting or down position, whichever is required by the particular exercise.

AKC Reg., Chapter 3, Section 12

THE FOUNDATION for the Stays rests on the control exercises; the thirty-minute Down, the ten-minute Sit and the five-minute Stand taught in the first eight weeks of training. For more information, see *Teaching Dog Obedience Classes: The Manual for Instructors*.

We look at the Stays from the perspective of time and distance. We first teach the dog to stay in place for a specific period of time with the handler about three feet in front of the dog. When distance is introduced, we reduce the time until the dog is steady. For example, Freddie has been taught a five-minute Sit Stay from three feet in front. The first time we increase the distance to six feet, we would only do a one-minute Sit Stay before returning to Freddie.

It is demonstrated by the following chart.

107

Distance	Time
3 feet	30 seconds
	1 minute
	2 minutes
	3 minutes
	4 minutes
	5 minutes
6 feet	1 minute
	2 minutes
	3 minutes
	4 minutes
	5 minutes
10 feet	1 minute
	2 minutes
	3 minutes
	4 minutes
	5 minutes
20 feet	1 minute
	2 minutes
	3 minutes
	4 minutes
	5 minutes

Each time there is a significant increase in distance, or when we introduce out of sight Stays, we reduce the time.

Most of what follows will be a review for you. Teaching Freddie the Stay consists of showing what to do, teaching him not to move and distraction training. If you have not attempted out of sight Stays, you can start at that point. If you have a stay problem, go through this chapter for ideas and perhaps steps you may have left out in your foundation training.

You can give your dog a command and/or signal. Unless the dog's Profile tells us otherwise, use both for the Stays. The Stay signal is given by bringing the right hand in front of your body to a point in front of your dog's nose and returning it to your side. It is a pendulumlike motion rather than a threat to swat Freddie.

Here is a brief overview of the progressions for the Stays.

SIT STAY

Sequence 1. Introduction

- With Freddie sitting at Heel, be sure the rings of the training collar are on top of his neck and the leash is attached to the dead ring.
- Neatly fold the leash into your left hand, hold it above his head and apply slight upward pressure on the collar, just enough so Freddie knows it's there and not enough to make him feel uncomfortable.
- Say and signal "Stay."
- Take a step to your right, count to ten, step back and release tension on the collar.
- Praise Freddie.
- Next, step directly in front of Freddie, count to ten and step back.
- Repeat ten times.

Sequence 2. Teaching your dog to stay

- With the rings of the collar under his chin, attach the leash to the live ring and neatly fold the leash in your left hand.
- Say and signal "Stay" and step three feet in front of Freddie.
- Place your left hand against your belt buckle and your right hand at your side, palm facing your dog.
- Carefully watch Freddie for signs of intentions to move, such as looking around or at the ground, or shifting.
- When he does, reinforce the Stay by taking a step toward him on your right leg and slapping the leash upward with the palm of your right hand to a point directly above his head.
- *Do not repeat* the "Stay" command. We want Freddie to learn it is his responsibility to concentrate on staying.

The most effective time to reinforce the Stay is when Freddie is thinking about moving and before he has a chance to do so. We *do not praise after* the slap on the leash because Freddie may still be thinking about moving. Praising him then

Reinforcing the Stay.

would only confuse him. You want him to think "Stay" and not encourage him to move.

Our preference is for Freddie to pay attention, and we reinforce the stay anytime he looks away from us.

Repeat over the course of several sessions until Freddie stays for five minutes without your having to reinforce.

Sequence 3. The Sit Stay test

- The leash should be on the dead ring of the collar, with the rings under his chin.
- Say and signal "Stay" and step three feet in front.
- Place your left hand (which holds the leash) against your belt buckle.
- Hold your right hand at your side, ready to reinforce.
- Rotate your left hand downward to apply a little pressure on the collar.
- If he tries to come to you, reinforce the stay and smile.
- Gradually increase the pressure until you see Freddie physically resisting.

The Sit Stay test is our basic review progression, and we use it from now on before doing a Stay.

Sequence 4. Introducing self-generated distractions

- Put the leash on the live ring of the collar, rings under his chin.
- Say and signal "Stay" and step three feet in front.
- Place your left hand against your belt buckle and hold your right hand ready to reinforce.

Teaching the Sit Stay and Sit Stay test.

- Jump to the right, the middle, the left, the middle, forward and backward. Any time Freddie wants to move, reinforce the stay. How vigorously you do these distractions depends on Freddie's Profile and your physical condition.

As he learns, add clapping and cheering. From your Novice experiences you will know that during the Stays there is almost always clapping and cheering going on around you, so you may as well prepare Freddie to stay when it happens.

Sequence 5. Other distractions

What you want Freddie to learn is that he has to concentrate on staying and not to listen to anybody else. For these distractions you need a helper.

- Leave Freddie on a sit stay and go three feet in front.
- Have your helper approach Freddie at a 45-degree angle.
- The helper should go to within one foot of him and tell Freddie to lie down by pointing to the ground. The dog's name is not used.
- If Freddie tries to lie down, reinforce the stay.
- Repeat until Freddie ignores your helper.

Your helper cannot be a member of your family because Freddie is supposed to obey him or her and you would hopelessly confuse the dog. In our case, we limit this type of distraction to a class setting, where the students act as each other's helpers. For more information about how these sequences are incorporated into a class setting consult *The Red Book*. (The Motivational Method—References).

For the next set of distractions, your helper encourages Freddie to come to him or her by saying, "Here, puppy, puppy, come visit." The helper also stands next to Freddie and tries to release him with "OK."

As Freddie becomes steady, other distractions, such as food or a ball, are introduced. Some of these you can do by yourself, such as placing a treat on the ground in front of Freddie or playing with a ball.

Sequence 6. Increasing distance

Work your way through sequences 2, 4, and 5 from six feet on leash, six feet off leash, ten feet off leash, etc.

When Freddie is off leash and you need to reinforce the stay, slowly approach him and put him back by placing two fingers of each hand through the collar at the side of his neck. If he is coming to you, put him back from in front. That is, guide him back to the spot where you left him in such as way that you are facing him when you reinforce the stay. The command is *not* repeated.

Sequence 7. Out of sight Stays

As an introduction to out of sight Stays, leave Freddie on a Sit Stay and go six feet in front of him. Pause for ten seconds, walk past him and stand six feet behind him with your back to him. Practice with distractions and have your helper tell you when Freddie moves and you have to reinforce the stay.

When you are ready to go out of sight, gradually increase the length of time you leave Freddie, starting with ten seconds.

Introduction to out of sight Stays with distractions.

DOWN STAY

Follow the same procedure for the Down Stay. As an added measure of safety, teach Freddie to lie on his left hip with his right paw tucked. It will help him concentrate on staying.

CAUTIONS

When teaching and practicing the Stays, we want to build Freddie's confidence. Some distractions are not worth the potential risk involved. For example, we do not recommend dropping a chair or banging pots and pans behind a line of dogs. It may literally ruin Freddie for life.

You will also have to practice the Stays without distractions in a quiet and sterile environment. Freddie has to learn to stay under those circumstances and without being entertained by a distractor.

Stays are a matter of confidence. Whining, for example, cannot be solved with compulsion. It will only make matters worse. If Freddie whines, work on building his confidence by rewarding the correct response. Leave him for ten seconds,

The first time the handlers go out of sight, it is to the count of ten before they return.

return and give him a treat or pet him, whatever his Profile calls for. If he is low in pack drive and high in prey, use a treat. If he is high in pack and low in prey drive, pet him by briefly massaging his shoulders.

Freddie's Profile will tell you what will work best with him.

THE YO-YO GAME

Some handlers have taught their dogs, or vice versa, what we call the yo-yo game. It goes something like this: Freddie is on a Sit Stay with handler standing thirty feet away. Freddie lies down, and handler approaches to reinforce the stay. Freddie sits up by himself and handler retreats. All is well in Obedience land, right? Not quite.

This scenario can, and often does, deteriorate into the yo-yo game. Freddie lies down, handler approaches, Freddie sits up, handler retreats, with Freddie not having learned a blessed thing, except perhaps the rules of the game and trying to figure out how many times he can play it.

Moral of the story: When you make a move—any move—to reinforce a command—any command—*you must follow through,* even if Freddie corrects himself before you have had a chance to reinforce the command.

PART III
Utility Training

10

Signal Exercise

The principal features of this exercise are the ability of dog and handler to work as a team while heeling, and the dog's correct responses to the signals to Stand, Stay, Drop, Sit and Come.

AKC Reg., Chapter 5, Section 5

WHEN YOU ARE TEACHING Heidi the Signal exercise, you will have to pay attention to her motivation and her position.

MOTIVATION

As we mentioned in Chapter 3, this is a control exercise. That is, it has a tendency to *de*motivate your dog. To avoid its potentially negative impact on Heidi's enthusiasm, we suggest practicing it with an object. For example, during the practicing phase, condition Heidi to do the down and sit with a treat or other object. Using a treat you can repeat the exercise many times in a row without losing her motivation.

Hold the object in the hand which gives the signal, and

give the object to Heidi only after she has dropped or sat quickly. Make a game of it anytime you want to give her a treat or just have some fun.

POSITION

The regulations require that your dog stand at heel position. If you started out using the Motivational Method, your dog already stands at heel. If not, you will have to teach her.

The Regulations also state that "minor or substantial deductions, depending on the specific circumstances in each case, shall be made for a dog that walks forward on the Stand, Drop or Sit portions of the exercise." In other words, you will have to teach Heidi to do the Drop and Sit in place, and without taking any steps. Keep this in mind as you go through the teaching sequences. We suggest that you focus on Heidi's front feet; it will tell you whether or not you are successful.

First progressions are important, if not critical, for any exercise, but especially this one. If you try to teach Heidi signals from long distance and she gets into the habit of walking forward in the process, you will have a hard time correcting the problem. Of course, you can accept such responses with the understanding that it will cost you points, perhaps all of them.

THE STAND, TEACHING YOUR DOG TO STAND AT HEEL

The signal is given with the left hand, from right to left, palm down and parallel to the ground, above and ahead of the dog's eyes.

- With Heidi sitting at Heel, off leash, place two fingers of your right hand, palm facing down, through her collar under her chin.
- Say "Stand."
- Take a step forward on your right leg as you draw her into a Stand at Heel position with your right hand, giving the signal with the left hand.
- Close with your left leg.

Stand at Heel.

- Praise and release.
- If necessary, support her rear end by placing your left hand against her right thigh.
- Repeat over the course of several sessions until your dog stands willingly.

When you draw Heidi forward with your right hand, remember that you want to teach her to stand at heel. You determine where she stands with your right hand. If you hold it against your left thigh and keep it there, Heidi will stand at heel.

STAND, FROM MOTION, ON LEASH

- With Heidi at Heel postion, leash in control position, say "let's go" and start walking.
- As you come to a halt and before you have closed your feet, put the leash in your right hand and place it against your left thigh.

121

- Say "Stand" and give the signal and make sure you stop her standing at Heel position.
- Praise and release with a treat.
- If necessary, support her rear end by placing your left hand against her right thigh.

Concentrate on putting your left hand against your left thigh so that Heidi cannot advance past Heel position. If you bring your right hand forward, Heidi will follow it and stand wherever you hold it. Repeat five times per session over the course of several sessions. After each stand praise and release enthusiastically with a treat. The object is to have Heidi Stand at Heel without any tension on the leash.

At some point, you may have to use a check to stop Heidi's forward momentum. If this becomes necessary, put the rings of her collar on top of her neck and just before you give the command, check Heidi straight back. Be sure the check is straight back. If you check up, you are telling her to sit.

The reinforcement for Standing at Heel is the check straight back. When you see Heidi getting a little ahead of you on the stand, start all over and stand her with a check. Do not try to check her back into Heel position once she has stood, as this will only confuse her. Just start all over.

STAND, OUT OF TURNS, ON LEASH

Repeat the exercises given for stand from motion, above, after a right turn, about turn and left turn. In the ring, you will get a stand right after a turn, so this is the maneuver you want to practice most.

STAND, FROM A FAST, ON LEASH

Teach Heidi the Stand from motion, above, from a fast pace. While not absolutely necessary, it is a good indicator how well Heidi knows this exercise, and a fun way to practice.

STAND, OFF LEASH

Review the Stands from motion, out of turns and from a fast, above, off leash.

Whether or not you teach Heidi the Stand as a separate exercise or combine it with the Drop and Sit is up to you. We don't want the dog to memorize the routine, but rather to respond to a specific command and in this case, signal. We like to vary the routine and combine the elements of the exercise on a random basis. A Stand need not be followed by a Drop, and a Drop need not be followed by a Sit. It has been our experience that dogs seem to be more motivated when they have to concentrate than when they are doing it by rote.

THE DOWN FROM THE STAND ON LEASH

The signal is given by bringing the right arm straight up above your shoulder as though you are reaching for the ceiling.

Down from Stand, in place.

123

- Stand Heidi at Heel position.
- Neatly fold the leash into your left hand.
- Say "Stay" and step in front of her.
- Kneel down and place two fingers of your left hand, palm facing down, through her collar, under the chin.
- Say "Down" and signal, at the same time pushing against her chest with your left hand.
- Then apply downward pressure on her collar. Tell her "Stay," stand up, praise and release with a treat.

The purpose of the pressure against the chest is to prevent her from moving her feet forward as she drops, the natural tendency for most dogs. You want to teach her collapse in place. Look at her feet as you drop her. With pressure against her chest, they will not move forward.

The downward pressure on the collar reinforces the drop. Be careful that you do not inadvertently pull her toward you, as that would make her come to you (take steps) as she drops.

Practice until she lies down in place without any pressure on her collar and without the command.

To save our backs, we taught this exercise to Ty, our Yorkshire Terrier, on a grooming table. If you have a small dog but no grooming table and want to try this, any table will do. Just put a mat on the table so your dog does not slip.

THE SIT FROM THE DOWN POSITION, ON LEASH

The signal is given with the right hand as follows:

- With your right arm hanging naturally at your side and with the back of the hand facing the dog, turn your hand so the palm faces your dog.
- Bring your arm out and away from your body, no higher than your waist, keeping your elbow locked. The object is to train your dog to respond to the turning of your hand. In the teaching phase, the arm moves in front of your body so it can slap the leash straight up.

124

Sit from Down, in place.

- Down your dog from a Stand, tell her to Stay and you stand up.
- Put your left hand, which holds the leash, against your right hip.
- Say "Sit" and with your right hand slap the leash straight up, palm up, to a point directly above her head, placing her into a Sit in place.
- Bring your hand back to your side.
- Praise and release with a treat.

The purpose of the slap on the leash is to have Heidi sit up in place *without* moving forward. You want her to bring her front feet up under her. Eliminate the command and practice until she anticipates the slap on the leash, that is, she sits when your hand turns.

Once Heidi responds correctly with your standing directly in front of her, you are ready to progress. The mechanics for the Down and Sit are the same.

DOWN AND SIT, FROM THREE FEET IN FRONT, ON LEASH

- As you give the signal, take a step toward Heidi with your right foot.
- Hold the signal until she has responded correctly.
- Then bring your leg and arm back to their original positions. The step toward Heidi reinforces the response in place and stops her from moving forward.
- Praise and give her a treat for every correct response.

DOWN AND SIT, FROM SIX FEET IN FRONT, ON LEASH

As you increase distance, it is important to continue with the step. Remember, her natural tendency is to come to you, and you want her to Drop and Sit in place.

DISTRACTIONS—ON LEASH

It is at this point in the training that we introduce distractions, beginning with **first degree**. The distractor stands ten feet from the dog, at a 45-degree angle.

After you have left Heidi on a Stand, the distractor approaches in a nonthreatening, benign manner within two feet of her. Give the signal to drop, with a step. If she does, praise and enthusiastically release. If she does not, *slowly* go to her and reinforce the down by putting two fingers of your right hand, the one that gave the signal, through her collar, under her chin. Place her down. When she does it correctly, praise, release with a treat, then stop and go on to something else.

At the next session, do the Drop and the Sit. Anytime you have to reinforce a response, use the opposite hand from the one that gave the signal and stop after the first correct response. The signal hand is used to reward the correct response.

For **second** and **third degree** distractions, the procedure is the same. You will have to assess how quickly you can progress and how important this is to you. The more distractible

126

Down from Stand, on leash, six feet in front, with distractor.

the dog, the more it needs distraction training. In the ring, you will be more than thirty feet from your dog and if Heidi is not paying attention there is nothing you can do. So now is the time to work on this.

You will have to make adjustments in accordance with Heidi's Profile. It tells you what you can expect and what you need to work on.

DOWN AND SIT, OFF LEASH

Stand about six feet in front of Heidi. Continue to use the step as you give the signal. Review with distraction before you increase distance. All this will go quickly, if you have a solid foundation. When she is reliable, combine with the Stand from motion.

In the meantime, make a game of this exercise in a non-training setting as often as you can. To keep her motivated, make it fun for Heidi.

Down from Stand, on leash, six feet in front, with third degree distraction.

THE COME, ON LEASH

- Leave Heidi on a Sit Stay and go to the end of the leash.
- With your left hand holding the leash at your left side, say "Come" *and* give the signal by bringing your right arm shoulder high and then to the center of your chest.
- Praise and release.
- After five repetitions, not necessarily in a row or at the same session, eliminate the command.

If Heidi does respond to the signal, give her a little tug on the leash. Praise and release. Practice until Heidi responds reliably to the signal.

COME, OFF LEASH

- Try Heidi off leash, from six feet in front.
- Praise and release.
- If she does not Come, show her by slowly going to her,

128

Hand signal . . .

for the Come.

put the leash on the dead ring of the collar, guide her in, praise and release.

From six feet away you cannot expect much speed. There is little motivation to come quickly for such a short distance. As soon as you increase distance, Heidi will pick up speed. Keep making it exciting for her by using a treat and the release.

SIGNAL TO FINISH

- If you finish Heidi to the right, step in front of her and hold the leash in your left hand placed, against your right hip.
- As you give the command, bring up your right hand and slap the leash in the direction you want her to go.
- Praise and release.
- If you want Heidi to finish to the left, reverse the pro-

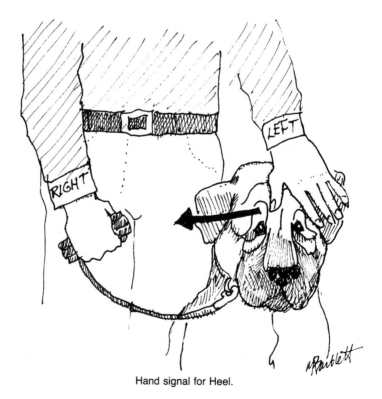

Hand signal for Heel.

cedure and hold the leash in your right hand, placed against your left hip.

- After five repetitions, eliminate the command.
- Practice until Heidi anticipates the slap on the leash and then try it off leash.

SIGNAL TO HEEL

- Hold the leash in your right hand.
- Give the command and signal by bringing your left hand forward around Heidi's head in a circular motion and then back to where you normally hold it.
- After five repetitions, eliminate the command.

11

Scent Discrimination

The principal features of these exercises are the selection of the handler's article from among other articles by scent alone, and the prompt delivery of the right article to the handler.

AKC Reg., Chapter 5, Section 7

TO A HANDLER the Scent Discrimination exercise can be exasperating because it is supposed to be simple for the dog. If it is so simple, then why is Basso not getting it? In all likelihood because you are confusing him or are making him anxious.

RULE 1. DO NOT SECOND GUESS YOUR DOG

Even after you think he knows it, Basso will make mistakes and bring back the wrong article; only he does not think so, otherwise he would not have brought it back. He may do this several times in a row, telling you he does not know the exercise as well as you thought. Just because he has done it correctly before, does not mean he is reliable.

Confusion

If it's so simple, then why is Basso not getting it?

Rule 1 dictates that you do nothing to discourage the dog. If you say no or do anything else to cause the dog to doubt the use of his nose—and you do this often enough—you will have a dog that is afraid to make a decision and will not pick up *any* article. For example, Basso may circle the articles and keep circling them until you give a second command and then he will pick up the nearest one.

RULE 2. KEEP YOUR COOL

Your feelings of frustration or anger will be picked up by Basso, who may then become anxious. If he does, he may either pick up the first article he comes to just to bring something back or do nothing at all. In either case, he will not be able to do the exercise correctly, and you better stop or you may set your training back several months.

What should you do if Basso brings back the wrong article? You definitely do not jump up and down yelling "no" at him. We suggest that before you do anything, you let him come back to you. Now you have two choices: you can either take the article from him and send him again, or you can repeat the command and send him back to the pile to try again.

While Basso is still learning the exercise, take the article from him and send him again. When he is further along in his training, repeat the command and see what he does. What you want him to do is go back to the pile, drop the wrong article and bring back the right one.

What you do *not* want to do is *interrupt* his return to send him to the articles again. It only takes a few times before this maneuver will cause Basso to hesitate on his return, return slowly or not at all without an extra command. Whatever he does, you want him to come to you briskly and with enthusiasm.

Although the Regulations do not require it, most handlers use metal and leather dumbbells for their articles. These can be either single, double or triple bar. With the double or triple bar, one of the bars may touch the dog under the chin, which some dogs do not like. Before investing in a set, borrow one from a friend and see how your dog responds. There is no point in making an issue out of the design of the articles, if you can avoid it. Ultimately, you should have two sets.

Introduce Basso to metal and leather articles. Having used the metal spoon with the Motivational Retrieve, Basso is already accustomed to having metal in his mouth, and leather is rarely a problem. Even so, he may refuse. Just because he retrieves his wooden dumbbell does not mean Basso will retrieve metal and leather. If he needs help, follow the same teaching progressions you used for his wooden dumbbell. When he retrieves either article reliably, you are ready to start this exercise.

THE GAME OF "FIND"

To teach Basso that you want him to use his nose, introduce him to the game of "find." For example, when training outside, hide the article around a corner. Let him see you take the article and return without it. Send him with "find it," and when he brings it back, release him backward with great enthusiasm and reward him with a treat. The first time you try this you may have to show him where you put the article. As he catches on, increase the difficulty so that he has to use his nose to find the article.

INTRODUCTION TO THE BOARD

A scent board can be a piece of pegboard commensurate with the size of your dog and large enough to accommodate the articles placed six inches apart. It can also be a piece of carpet or rubber matting.

- Accustom Basso to walking on the board by heeling him over it several times.
- Have him sit on it.
- Then have him retrieve an article from the board, first by throwing it on the board, and then by placing it.
- Release backward and reward.

It is important that Basso is comfortable retrieving from the board before you begin to add other articles.

Prepare the board for the next sequence by tying one of each article on the board, with the tie underneath, and with anywhere from one half to six inches of slack. Let the board air out for twenty-four hours to become devoid of scent.

SCENT ARTICLES

Make sure your hands are clean and free from chemicals and perfumes. During hot and humid weather scent is easily retained by the article, and just the opposite is the case in cold weather. There are no hard-and-fast rules about how long you should handle the article, and you will have to let experience be your guide. In familiar locations we scent the article for ten seconds, and in unfamiliar location, for twenty.

- Start with both you and Basso facing the board from ten feet away.
- Scent a metal article by slowly rubbing the bar for twenty seconds.
- Say "find it" and let Basso briefly hold it.
- Take the article and let him watch you place it on the board closest to him.
- Return and send him.

If Basso tries to pick up an incorrect article encourage him to keep looking saying "you can do it" in an excited tone of voice or anything other than the original command. When he picks up the correct one, quietly say "that's it," with a big

Let Basso see you place it on the board.

smile on your face, release backward and reward. Let Basso know he did the right thing when he picks up the article and reserve your main reward and praise for having returned.

Repeat by placing the scented leather article in a different location on the board until you are sure Basso is using his nose to find the correct article. At the same time, gradually increase the distance you stand from the board to twenty feet. During this sequence stop the praise for picking up the correct article, but continue to smile. You don't want Basso to become dependent on praise and wait for it before he returns, so get rid of it as soon as you can. Release and reward Basso after he has returned. Stop after two successive successful responses, that is, one metal and one leather.

Tie two more articles on the board, varying the length of slack for each article. After each successful round, tie two more articles on the board until eight articles are tied on the board. As you add new articles, you may have to encourage Basso. During the entire teaching process, you and your dog are facing the articles.

If Basso appears to be dense about this exercise and does not seem to catch on, put the board in a dark room and try again. One problem we have often seen is the effect of medication taken by either the handler or the dog on the dog's ability to do this exercise. Since medication wears off, its impact waxes and wanes, which can cause confusion.

Our Lab, Bean, is a compulsive retriever and he would jump onto the board, frantically trying to retrieve whatever he came to first. To slow him down, we put him on a down, one foot in front of the board and then sent him. It slowed him down long enough to figure out the object of the exercise.

Other dogs walk to the articles at this stage, which is not an unusual response. They are still trying to learn, and there is little to be gained by attempts to speed them up. Speed comes with confidence.

Some dogs develop a preference—usually for leather—and will go to great lengths to avoid picking up the metal article. We deal with this by using only metal articles until the dog is reliable, and then reintroduce leather.

DISCRIMINATION

Up until now, Basso has only learned to find your article among unscented ones. The object of the exercise is to teach him to find your article among those that have been touched by someone else. Before you send Basso, have a helper briefly touch the articles on the board, then place yours. You and Basso are still facing the board.

Some dogs catch on quickly, and others need to go back to the beginning with two articles tied down. You will have to experiment with Basso to see how he does. Try it with all eight articles tied down. If he gets hopelessly confused, start at the beginning.

DISTRACTIONS

When Basso is reliable at this step, distractions are introduced. Have a distractor stand about two feet from the articles (first degree) and send Basso. As Basso gains confidence in his ability to perform this exercise, gradually increase the level of difficulty over the course of several training sessions by having the distractor stand in the pile, then crouch in the pile; then

Distractor stands two feet from the board.

go to second degree distractions, and finally to third degree. As a general rule, we ony do one distraction per session and stop after each successful round. The object is not to continue until Basso makes a mistake, but to build his confidence.

WEANING BASSO FROM THE BOARD

To wean him from the board, reverse the procedure and untie two articles. After each successful round, stop. Over the course of several sessions, repeat until all the articles are loose on the board.

Doing this exercise on the board and doing it on any other surface are not the same. You can either work with the board and place two articles on the ground and as Basso is successful, place the remainder, two at a time, on the ground in front of the board. You can also start again with just two articles on the ground and build from there. Once he is proficient at this part of the exercise, use the same procedure to move the articles from the board onto grass and rubber matting. However, it is unwise to go from the board to another surface without some transition. Our Dachshund, Demi, got hopelessly confused

Distractor stands on the board.

when we placed all the articles on grass directly from the board. We had to start again with two and build from there.

Right after it looks as though Basso has finally gotten the hang of it, he may go through one or more regressions—he gives the appearance of not having the foggiest idea of what this exercise is all about. You can recognize this by the number of successive incorrect responses. Basso brings back the wrong article, you send him back again and he brings back another incorrect article, and so on. This is normal and you should expect it. The best advice we can give you is to put him back on the board for several days as a form of review.

For quick success the key is to stick to the rules. Don't second guess your dog and keep your cool! Under no circumstances reprimand Basso in any way, shape or form for bringing back an incorrect article. If you do, you will undermine his confidence in his ability to use his nose, and, done often enough, will cause him to stop trying altogether. The withholding of praise is more than enough to let him know something went wrong. Look at it this way: Every time you lose your cool, you will set your training back by one month.

Weaning your dog off the board.

TURN AND SEND

At this point you are ready to introduce the Turn and Send. You may turn either to the left or the right. For teaching the turn in place, see Directed Retrieve.

- With Basso at Heel, stand with your back to the articles.
- Make an about turn in place, saying "Basso, Heel" to face the articles.
- Send him with "find it."
- Remember, the Sit at Heel after the turn in place is scored just like any other Sit at Heel.

Some handlers like to give their scent to the dog by touching the dog's nose with the palm of the hand before they make the turn. There is a theory which says that filling the dog's nose with your scent makes the exercise harder for the dog because he first has to clear his nose. Whether or not this is so, we cannot answer. We ourselves have always felt that surely by

140

Directed Retrieve: introducing . . .

direction.

142

12

Directed Retrieve

*The principal features of the exercise are that the dog
stay until directed to retrieve, that it go directly to the
designated glove and that it retrieve promptly.*

AKC Reg., Chapter 5, Section 9

FOR THIS EXERCISE Cassie will need to know
how to turn in place and how to retrieve a designated glove.
If you started with the Motivational Method, Cassie already
knows how to turn in place. If you did not, you will have to
teach her. Following is a quick review of the sequences we use.
When working on the turns in place, keep in mind that the
more accurate your dog is on Heel position, the less likely she
will make a mistake.

RIGHT TURN IN PLACE

1. **Placing the right foot**—With your dog at Heel, leash
in control position (in both hands, with no more than a half
inch of slack, left hand close to the leash snap), place your
right foot at a 90-degree angle one large step to the right. Say

143

Diagram for the right turn in place.

"Cassie, Heel," close with your left foot and guide your dog into heel position. Praise and release. Repeat twenty-five times over several sessions.

2. **With a large step**—With your dog at Heel, leash in control position, say "Cassie, Heel," take a step to the right, close with the left and guide your dog into heel position. Praise and release. Repeat twenty-five times over several sessions.

3. **Right turn in place**—Say "Cassie, Heel," and turn in place to the right. Praise and release.

RIGHT ABOUT TURN IN PLACE

1. **Two steps forward, turn, two steps forward**—With your dog at heel, leash in control position, say "Cassie, Heel," take two steps forward and make an about turn to your right. Keeping your feet together, take two steps forward, guiding your dog into heel position. Praise and release. Repeat twenty-five times.

2. **One step forward, turn, one step forward**—Say "Cassie, Heel," take one step forward. Turn and take one step forward, guiding your dog into heel position. Praise and release. Repeat twenty-five times over several sessions.

Right turn . . .   in place.

145

3. **Right about turn in place**—Say "Cassie, Heel," and make two right turns in place, guiding your dog into Heel position. Praise and release.

LEFT TURN IN PLACE

1. **Large step**—With your dog at Heel, leash in control position, place your left foot directly in front of your dog's front feet. Say "Cassie, heel" and take a large step with your right foot past the left. Close with the left, guiding your dog into heel position with slight backward pressure on the leash. Praise and release. Repeat twenty-five times over several sessions.

2. **Small step**—Place your left foot directly in front of your dog's front feet. Say "Cassie, Heel" and take a small step with your right foot past your left. Close with the left, guiding your dog into heel position with slight backward pressure on the leash. Praise and release. Repeat twenty-five times.

3. **In place**—With your dog at Heel, say "Cassie, Heel," put your right foot at a 90-degree angle directly in front of your left (in a *T* shape). Guide your dog into Heel position with slight backward pressure on the collar. Praise and release. Repeat twenty-five times.

LEFT ABOUT TURN IN PLACE

Say "Cassie, Heel" and make two left turns in place, guiding your dog into Heel position with slight backward pressure on the collar. Praise and release.

TEACHING THE GLOVES

1. Giving the direction—Obedience regulations permit you to send your dog as you give the direction. They also permit you to mark the direction and then send Cassie for the glove. This is what we teach. The direction is given by holding the left arm at the side of the dog's head, with the hand, fingers pointing straight toward the glove, held ahead of her nose. Immediately

Preparing for the . . .

left turn . . .

in place.

Right foor in front of left (*T*) . . .   for the left turn in place.

following the giving of the direction, the com mand to take it is given. What you may *not* do is give Cassie the direction and then pump your let arm as you tell her to take it.

For the center glove, the arm is stretched out so that the elbow is in line with the dog's nose. You may bend your body and knees to the extent necessary in giving the direction to your dog. When giving the direction, make sure your fingers are indeed pointing at the designated glove. For reasons not clear to me I had developed the habit of marking the direction with my fingers bent and then straightening them with the command to point at the designated glove. Not only could this throw off the dog, but it was a double command. Fortunately, someone caught me before this became a problem.

2. Introduce direction—With your dog sitting at Heel, and a glove in your left hand held between thumb and fingers, get Cassie excited about the glove. Throw the glove, holding your arm as you would if you were to mark the glove, and tell her "take it." After she has picked it up, praise and release. If she does not retrieve, reveiw teaching her to retrieve.

3. Placing the gloves—Once your dog retrieves the glove and you have introduced her to the direction, place a glove fifteen feet to your right, fifteen feet to your left and fifteen

148

Placing the gloves.

Giving the direction for number two.

feet in front of you. Say, "Cassie, Heel" and make a right turn in place. Have Cassie face the glove on your right. Mark the direction with your left arm. You may have to hold on to Cassie by placing two fingers of your right hand through her collar. Send your dog with the command "take it." Praise and release after she has picked up the glove.

Repeat for the glove on the left, and the center glove. After three successful repetitions, move the gloves on your right and left, two feet straight forward and start all over. After each set of three successful repetitions, move the gloves on your right and left two feet straight forward until they are in line with the center glove. Send Cassie to different gloves in a random pattern.

149

CORRECTING MISTAKES

What if she goes to the wrong glove? We let her try to work it out for herself by maintaining the signal.

For example, Cassie goes to number two instead of number one. Hold the signal facing number one. When Cassie returns to you she immediately notices something is wrong—you are not standing up straight but are still pointing to the glove. She may try to do one of several things: insist on giving you the glove, which you do not take; give up and do nothing or go for another glove, probably the correct one.

If she retrieves the correct glove, stand up, praise and release. If she does nothing, approach the number one glove, still holding the signal, and get her to pick it up, preferably just by pointing at it and without an extra command. When she does, praise and release. If she does not, reinforce the retrieve.

The key to letting Cassie work it out for herself is patience. We do not interfere until we are certain Cassie has stopped working. As long as it looks as though there is activity in that brain, we give her a chance.

Every time you help Cassie you are assuming the responsibility for her behavior. You want her to learn that it is her responsibility. To do that you have to be able to give her a chance to work it out for herself.

Introduce distractions the same way as for other exercises. Should Cassie go to the wrong glove to avoid the distractor, use one distractor for each glove.

Once Cassie has learned the direction portion of the exercise, you can introduce the Turn and Send.

The Regulations permit you to turn *either* to the left or to the right, and you will have to experiment what is best for you and Cassie. Some dogs "lock in" on the first glove they spot during the turn. For example, if you turn to the right for number two and Cassie locks in on number one during the turn, that is the one she may want to retrieve. For this reason many handlers turn to the left for number two, to reduce the chance of the dog spotting another glove during the turn.

Whichever way you turn, you must face the designated glove or you will be subject to a penalty. Cassie must also Sit at Heel after the turn, and you must turn in place.

13

Moving Stand
and Examination

---

*The principal features of the exercise are that the dog
heel, stand and stay on command by the moving handler, accept the examination without shyness or resent-
ment and, on command, return to the handler.*

AKC Reg., Chapter 5, Section 11

THIS EXERCISE consists of standing still on
command, an examination and going to Heel from about ten
feet in front. Caesar already knows almost the entire exercise.
He knows how to Stand at Heel and only has to learn to Stay
while you continue walking. The Examination is an extension
of the Novice Stand for Examination and is done as "in dog
show judging." He also has to learn to go to Heel not from
directly in front but from ten feet.

SIGNAL AND COMMAND TO STAND AND STAY, ON LEASH

- With your dog on leash and at heel, say "let's go" and start walking.
- After several steps, give the signal to Stand, say "Stay" and continue walking.
- When you get to the end of the leash, turn and face your dog.
- Tell Caesar what a clever fellow he is.
- Count to five and release.

If Caesar needs help, use the same technique to teach him to Stand and Stay which you used to teach him the Stand at Heel.

Signal and command to Stand and Stay, on leash.

152

SIGNAL AND COMMAND FROM FAST, ON LEASH

Repeat the sequence for signal and command to Stand and Stay, above, from a fast pace.

SIGNAL AND COMMAND, OFF LEASH

Repeat the sequence for signal and command to Stand and Stay, above, off leash.

GOING TO HEEL, ON LEASH

- After several steps, stand your dog, go to the end of the leash and face him.
- Count to five, then signal and say "Basso, Heel," guiding him into Heel position.
- Praise and release. The regulations permit you to give both the signal and the command to Heel.

GOING TO HEEL, OFF LEASH

- Repeat off leash.
- Over the course of several training sessions, gradually increase the distance you leave Caesar on a stand until you can go about ten to twelve feet, as required by the Regulations, before you turn and face him.

THE EXAMINATION

- After several steps, stand your dog and continue walking for ten to twelve feet.
- Turn and face your dog.
- Have a helper examine him and then call him to Heel.

It is usually not necessary to go through distraction training for this exercise because the examination is a form of dis-

Going to Heel, off leash.

The examination.

154

traction. What you do have to watch is that Caesar does not start to anticipate the stand while heeling. Should this happen to you, examine what you do with the left side of your body— you may inadvertently make some motion, which is interpreted by Caesar as an intention on your part to give the Stand signal.

For some time, Caesar may also go through a period of confusion whether or not he should sit front or finish on the returns. If he experiences this uncertainty, it will manifest itself in crooked fronts. Since he is not sure whether to sit front or finish, a logical solution is somewhere in the middle. As he gains confidence in what he is doing, this will disappear.

Directed jumping: Sequence 2- Introducing . . .

direction.

14

Directed Jumping

---

*The principal features of this exercise are that the dog
go away from the handler in the direction indicated,
stop when commanded, jump as directed and return as
in the Recall*

AKC Reg., Chapter 5, Section 13

W̲E APPROACH this exercise in three parts:
the go-out, the jumping and putting the two together. The first
two parts are taught at the same time, but not together. For
example, the go-out is taught without reference to the jumps.
When Diggy has learned the go-out and the directed jumping
part, we then put them together.

GO-OUT

To teach Diggy to leave, we use food or an object such
as a stick or a toy. To teach her where to go, we use a chute,
made from two boards of the Broad Jump, set on end.

Make the chute wide enough so that your dog can comfortably turn in it. You will find that as you increase distance,

the chute is as much a visual aid to you in deciding whether or not she has gone far enough as it is for your dog. In addition, we put the chute in front of a barrier, such as a section of fencing, a fence or the side of a house. Before sending Diggy into the chute, get her used to it by heeling her into the chute and then by calling her into it.

Introduce target and chute

- Put a target, commensurate with the size of your dog, inside the chute.
- With Diggy on leash, show her a treat and say "out," as *both of you go* into the chute.
- Place the treat on the target and let her pick it up.
- Praise, encourage her to turn around in the chute and release her.
- Teach her to turn in the chute.
- Do not let her jump out of the chute.
- Repeat until Diggy is comfortable with going into and turning in the chute.

Go-out: Showing your dog where to go.

158

Let your dog see you place the treat.

Next:

- Leave Diggy on a Sit Stay ten feet in front of the target.
- Let her see you place a treat on the target.
- Go back to Heel position and send her with "Diggy, out." You may signal her (at the same time) with the left hand in the direction you want her to go.
- When she gets to the target, let her take the treat, praise and call her back.
- With each successive repetition, increase the distance to the target by two feet until you are seventy-five feet from the target.
- Repeat at that distance fifty times over the course of several sessions.

Eliminate the target

- Remove the target.
- Leave Diggy on a Sit Stay, ten feet from the barrier.
- Go into the chute, point to the ground and go back to heel position.
- Send your dog.
- After she has left, quietly follow her so that when she gets to the spot you indicated, you are at the entrance to the chute.

Send your dog and . . .

let her pick up the treat.

- Say "Diggy, Sit," using the Sit hand signal and a step forward to make her sit in place.
- Reward her with a treat, held in the hand which gave the signal. From now on, Diggy is only rewarded for going to the designated spot and she has to learn that the reward comes from you.

Go-out: Eliminate the target, point to the ground . . .

send your dog . . .

With each successive repetition, increase the distance to the target by two feet until you are seventy-five feet from the target. Repeat at that distance fifty times over the course of several sessions.

It is during this progression that Diggy learns to turn and sit in the chute. Continue to follow her and use the step *and* signal so that she understands you want her to turn and sit immediately. The step and signal prevent her from getting into

quietly follow her . . .

say "Diggy, Sit" with step and signal, and . . .

the habit of taking several steps back toward you, which you don't want.

If Diggy does not leave or only goes part of the way, without saying anything, slowly approach her, put two fingers of your left hand through the collar, back to front, palm facing you, at the side of her neck and take her to the spot you indicated. Reinforce the sit with the command "Sit." Let go, give her a treat and release. Send her again.

162

give her a treat.

Diggy also has to learn that she has to keep going until you tell her to sit. The Regulations provide that substantial deductions shall be made for a dog that "turns, stops or sits before the handler's command." Insist that she go into the chute. Responses such as going to the entrance of the chute or going partly into the chute are not acceptable.

This exercise can quickly deteriorate, if you get lazy about it. If Diggy takes an inch in practice, that can become several feet in the ring. During times of stress, minor mistakes can become major mistakes.

Working on the Sit

- Start again at the beginning from ten feet away.
- Point to the spot, send your dog, but stay where you are.
- When Diggy gets to the spot you indicated, say "Diggy, Sit."
- After she has sat, go to her and give her a treat.
- Then release.
- Repeat, increasing the distance with each successive repetition, until she sits in the chute on command from seventy-five feet away. The chute shows you clearly which responses are acceptable and which ones are not.

Go-out: Use step and signal so . . .

she sits in the chute.

If Diggy does not leave or only goes part of the way, without saying anything, slowly approach her, put two fingers of your left hand through the collar, back to front, palm facing you, at the side of her neck and take her to the spot you indicated. Reinforce the Sit with "Sit," let go, give her a treat and release. Send her again.

Sending your dog twice

- Leave Diggy on a Sit Stay.
- You go into the chute, point to the spot and go back to Heel position.

164

- Send her and when she gets to the spot, say "Diggy, Sit."
- Praise, count to five, release and call her back to you.
- Line her up at Heel position and send her again.
- When she gets there have her Sit.
- Go to her, praise, reward and release.
- Repeat this sequence fifty times over several sessions.

If she does not leave you or does not go to the designated spot, show her where you want her to go.

Reducing the size of the chute

When Diggy goes into the chute reliably and sits on command, you can reduce the size of the chute. We use what we call "snakes"—two pieces of rope, about two feet long.

- First get Diggy used to her new chute.
- Then review the last three sequences.
- Since she already has a good idea what this exercise is all about, this will go quickly.

Combining the go-out with the jumps

After you have taught Diggy the Directed Jumping, you will be ready to combine the go-out with the jumps, which will become her guides.

Reducing the size of the chute with "snakes."

In practice, leave the chute in place at all times. Remove the chute only when you are testing. The first few times you remove the chute, go to the spot where you want her to go before you send her.

Distraction training

Introduce distractions as you have for previous exercises by having the distractor first stand midway between you and the designated spot, two feet from Diggy's line of travel, and then two feet from the designated spot. Work your way through first, second and third degree distractions. If Diggy bows away from the distractor, use two distractors, starting at eight feet apart, and teach her to go straight through.

THE BAR JUMP AND THE SOLID JUMP

Introducing the bar

- Introduce Diggy to the Bar Jump which should be set at teaching height (the height of your dog at her elbows).
- Walk her up to the jump, on a leash attached to the dead ring.
- Touch the bar with your left hand.
- Let her investigate the jump.
- Start from ten feet away, say "bar" and briskly walk toward the jump.
- Let her jump as you go over with her or around the jump.
- Repeat until she jumps without any hesitation.

Introducing direction

Set up the High Jump (Solid Jump) and the Bar Jump at teaching height, two feet apart.

- Leave Diggy on a Sit Stay, ten feet back from the center of the Bar Jump.
- You go over the jump, focus her attention on the bar by touching it and, from ten feet back, face the upright of the Bar Jump.
- Say "bar" as you give the signal by bringing your arm

up from your side to shoulder height and pointing toward the jump.

- At the same time take a step toward the jump.
- As she commits herself to jump, lower your arm and close your leg.
- Praise as she lands and release.
- Now have her go over the High Jump (solid) using the word "jump."
- Repeat several times.

For the next teaching step, place Diggy on a Sit Stay ten feet from and facing the upright of the jump.

- You go over the jump and focus her attention on the jump.
- Stand ten feet back from and in the center **between the jumps**.
- Send her with command "bar" or "jump," with a signal and step.

Now leave her on a Sit Stay, ten feet from the center **between the jumps**.

- You go over the jump and focus her attention.
- Stand in the center between the jumps, ten feet from the center line between the jumps.
- Face your dog, and send her with "bar" or "jump."

Separating the jumps

When Diggy goes over the correct jump reliably, begin separating the jumps in two-foot increments. **Continue to step over the one you want her to jump,** focus her attention on the jump, signal and step. Each time you separate the jumps, position your dog and yourself an additional foot from the center line so that when the jumps are eighteen feet apart, your dog and you are each twenty feet from the center line, respectively. When you have reached that point, eliminate the step.

Raising the jumps

Begin raising the jumps in two- or four-inch increments, depending on the size of your dog. If the height becomes an issue, put the jumps closer together before separating them

Directed jumping: Sequence 3- Separating the jumps.

again. Difficulties with jumping are never disciplinary in nature; your dog is trying to tell you something. Listen to her!

PUTTING IT ALL TOGETHER

You are now ready to combine the go-out with the directed jumping.

- Put your small chute in front of the fence and leave Diggy midway between the two jumps.
- Go into the chute and point to the spot where you want her to go.

Putting it all together.

168

- You return to Heel position.
- Send her out and tell her to sit and stay.
- Go back to the spot from which you are going to send her over the jumps.
- Give the command and signal to jump.
- Praise as she lands and release.
- Repeat for the other jump.

Now start with Diggy at Heel position, two feet back from the center line between the jumps and follow the same procedure. Repeat in two-foot increments until you stand at the appropriate spot for the exercise before sending your dog. Following this procedure the first few times you put the go-out together with the directed jumping is a precaution. It should prevent Diggy from coming up with the idea, as she otherwise might, that she has to jump on the way out.

After every two go-outs, reinforce that exercise with five repetitions into the chute, the first, third and fifth rewarded by a treat.

CONCLUSION

What should you do when Diggy makes a mistake and goes over the wrong jump? Try letting her work it out. Maintain your signal and wait. The response you want to see is Diggy going back to the go-out spot without any help or command from you. When she does, lower your arm, tell her to sit and repeat the signal.

Suppose she does nothing and just sits in front of you not knowing what to do. Give her a chance until you are absolutely certain that she has stopped trying, then take her back to where she started, leave her, return and send her again.

Seeing a dog go through the "aha" response—that is, Diggy shows you that she has figured out what you want—is perhaps one of the most exciting aspects of training a dog. To get there, **you must never discourage your dog from trying,** even if the response is incorrect. Permit and encourage your dog to solve these training problems and you will have a motivated student.

Obedience exhibitor.

Epilogue

OBEDIENCE COMPETITION is a wonderful sport. Whatever your goal—to qualify or to be High in Trial—you can reach that goal. From casual participant to pro, you can be a winner. Few leisure activities have so many rewards.

Obedience competition is not a matter of life and death. It is a sport, and all the rules of good sportsmanship apply. Win with grace and lose with grace. Above all, remember why you have your dog and who is responsible for the training.

Using the Motivational Method, most dogs are perfectly willing to go along with the program. Give them a chance by treating them fairly and with consistency.

When you experience what you perceive to be a problem, ask yourself, "What is my responsibility toward its solution?" We start with the basic premise that it is rarely the dog's fault. If you do the same, the solution will come to you.

References for the Motivational Method

Volhard, Jack, and Melissa Bartlett. *What All Good Dogs Should Know: The Sensible Way to Train.* New York: Howell Book House, 1991.

Volhard, Jack, and Wendy Volhard. *Motivational Retrieve: Teaching, Practicing, Testing* (videotape). New York: Top Dog Training School, 1991.

Volhard, Jack, and Wendy Volhard. *Utility Training: The Teaching Phase* (videotape). New York: Top Dog Training School, 1990.

Volhard, Jack, and Wendy Volhard. *Open Training: The Teaching Phase* (videotape). New York: Top Dog Training School, 1990.

Volhard, Jack, and Wendy Volhard. *The Red Book: Lesson Plans & Homework Sheets for Puppies & Beginners, Intermediate & Novice, 8 weeks each.* New York: Top Dog Training School, 1990.

Volhard, Jack, and Wendy Volhard. *Foundations Training: Level I* (videotape). Durham: Green Light Creations, 1988.

Volhard, Wendy. *Back to Basics: A Guide to a Balanced Home-made Dog Food.* New York: Top Dog Training School, 1988.

Volhard, Joachim J., and Gail T. Fisher. *Teaching Dog Obedience Classes: The Manual for Instructors.* New York: Howell Book House, 1986.

Volhard, Joachim J., and Gail T. Fisher. *Training Your Dog: The Step-by-Step Manual.* New York: Howell Book House, 1983.

Publications available from:
Top Dog Training School
R.D. 1, Box 518
Phoenix, NY 13135

Bibliography

Bergman, Goran. *Why Does Your Dog Do That?* New York: Howell Book House, 1973.

Lorenz, Konrad. *Man Meets Dog.* New York: Penguin Books, 1964.

Lorenz, Konrad. *On Aggression.* New York: Harcourt, Brace & World, Inc., 1966.

Most, Konrad. *Training Dogs.* London: Popular Dogs, 1954.

Pfaffenberger, Clarence J. *The New Knowledge of Dog Behavior.* New York: Howell Book House, 1963.

Pryor, Karen. *Lads Before the Wind.* New York: Harper & Row, 1975.

Volhard, Joachim J. and Gail T. Fisher. *Training Your Dog: The Step-by-Step Manual.* New York: Howell Book House, 1983.

Volhard, Joachim J., and Gail T. Fisher. *Teaching Dog Obedience Classes: The Manual for Instructors.* New York: Howell Book House, 1986.